SMALL BUSINESS

BIG MONEY ONLINE

A PROVEN SYSTEM TO OPTIMIZE ECOMMERCE WEBSITES
AND INCREASE INTERNET PROFITS

ALEX HARRIS

FOREWORD BY BRYAN EISENBERG

Printed in the United States of America
By Alex Harris, AlexDesigns.com

ISBN: 0692466037
ISBN-13: 978-0692466032

ADVANCED PRAISE FOR
SMALL BUSINESS, BIG MONEY ONLINE

Please take the time to read this book. You can learn a lot from Alex Harris. He is not one of the many Johnny-come-lately charlatans so popular in the conversion rate optimization market. He is not simply spouting opinions or regurgitating questionable best practices. Alex knows what works and what doesn't from real world experience. He is a proven veteran conversion rate optimization warrior with a decade of big wins under his belt. We've recommended him more times than we can count, and we've successfully included him on our projects since 2004. You cannot go wrong when learning from or working with Alex.

~**Jeffrey Eisenberg,** author of *Buyer Legends: The Executive Storyteller's Guide*

Alex is one of the few people in the industry that values and understands the impacts that design can have on conversion. It's a rare trait to have in a conversion optimizer and by association the knowledge he shares in his book has a ton of value.

~**Oli Gardner,** co-founder of *Unbounce*

Alex is one of the rare, true conversion-oriented designers. Every small business owner should read this and follow everything it says. Don't wait. Start now.

~**Chris Goward,** Founder of WiderFunnel and Author of *You Should Test That!*

Reading this book may be the highest ROI activity you ever perform.

~**Lance Loveday,** founder of *Closed Loop* and author of *Web Design for ROI*

Conversion optimization is the key to success on the web and Alex Harris is an expert when it comes to conversion rate optimization. If your business depends on your website, then you're bound to listen to what Alex Harris has to say. Based on his deep experience and backed by sound conversion optimization principles, his system will help make your website soar. I definitely recommend taking Alex's advice on reading his book. Anyone that does and puts his system into practice will get real results that help generate real revenue for their business.

~ **Morgan Brown,** Head of Growth at *Qualaroo*

If you want customers to open their wallets, you need to open your eyes and ears to the psychology of e-commerce. Alex's book gives you an array of processes for optimizing conversion, but along the way it does something more important. Small Business, Big Money Online will convert the way you approach e-commerce.

~**Barry Feldman**, founder of *Feldman Creative Online*

Concise, crisp and actionable across any industry. Great framework to guide one on the path of the CRO Journey.

~**Tejaswi Chawla**, Vice President-Global Sales of *Visual Website Optimizer*

Alex gets optimization. He isn't a journalist or 'researcher' who simply reports on relatively shallow industry trends, but actually does the incredibly difficult optimization work first hand. Alex understands the optimization process probably better than most people I know, and he is sharing exactly how he helps grow businesses with his own optimization model. This book is a must read for both newbies and veterans alike, so stop reading his praises and start reading the book already!

~**Justin Rondeau,** Conversion Optimization Manager at *Digital Marketer*

In order to succeed online, you must dedicate resources to conversion optimization. But it's not enough to simply run some A/B tests; you have to follow a system in order to get substantial results. In this book, Alex outlines a system that any company can - and should - follow in their optimization efforts. Read this, follow his system, and prosper!

~**Theresa Baiocco,** founder of *ConversionMax.com*

Alex has been an inspiration to me. I'm happy to know him as a conversion optimization colleague and as a friend. He continues to stay on the forefront of the industry and approaches optimization with a structured rigorous process that's been refined over the years through real world trial and error. He's one of the better CRO practitioners out there.

~**Bobby Hewitt,** CEO & President of *Creative Thirst.*

There are too many people out there who pay lip service to the business of conversion rate optimization but don't understand how to do it properly. Alex Harris isn't one of them. This guy is one of the few who truly knows what he's talking about. Between listening to his podcasts and reading his books, I've been able to bring new insights to my own clients. I count Alex as one of my mentors.

If you want to learn what it means to go through the CRO process thoughtfully and strategically, read this book. Alex lays it all out for you with case studies to boot. You'll get an inside look at how an expert optimizes a site. Lots of takeaways and super actionable! It's definitely worth the price of admission.

~**Jen Havice,** owner of *Make Mention Media LLC*

If you're competing in the e-commerce game these days, you need to execute on multiple fronts at the same time. It can be overwhelming. The best thing you can do is find a few resources you can trust and focus on learning from their experience and how you can use it to grow your business. Alex Harris is one of those few resources you should trust, and his new book brings you an incredible amount of value that will have a tremendous impact on your business.

~**Jordan Gal,** Founder & CEO of *CartHook.*

Alex is one of those people that have the experience to back up writing a book. With over a decade of experience helping businesses, all of his advice is proven and tested over and over again. The strategies and examples are easy to follow, and if you take action, you can get quick results from Alex's advice.

~Jason Swenk, founder of *JasonSwenk.com*

Alex is my go-to guy for all things conversion-optimization. I know I can count on him for honest data-driven feedback and concrete results. If you'd like to generate more leads and sales from your website (and who doesn't??), this book gives you a step-by-step system to make it happen.

~Nick Loper, author of *Work Smarter: 500+ Online Resources Today's Top Entrepreneurs Use to Increase Productivity and Achieve Their Goals* and founder of *SideHustleNation.com*

Alex is a beast when it comes to conversion rate optimization. He doesn't share theories and hypotheticals, he shares first-hand knowledge about how you can optimize your presence to increase leads and sales. Get your pen and paper ready, because Alex is about to share some serious knowledge.

~Steve P Young, founder of *Appmasters.co*

Alex is an invaluable leader and pioneer in our rapidly growing field of Marketing Optimization. Having trained with the best and mastered his craft, his commitment to sharing his experiences and educating all of us is second to none. Newcomers and experienced practitioners alike will benefit greatly from the insights and wisdom in his podcast and books.

~Arun Sivashankaran, Founder & Chief Optimizer of *Funnel Envy*

"Small Business Big Money Online" is a one-stop shop for anyone who's creating an e-commerce website. And if you wanna optimize it so you can increase your Internet profit, you definitely wanna check it out. Not only does he provide some great action steps throughout the books, but there's also case studies so you can learn from real world examples out there. I definitely highly recommend this book. Check it out.

~Anthony Tran, founder of *Marketing Access Pass*

Alex Harris has become a leading authority in conversion rate optimization and with his book, "Small Business Big Money Online," he absolutely proves it. So there are a few things that I look for in a book like this that they have to include: number one is that it has to have some kind of track record. Well, with over a decade of experience, Alex definitely has that. The next thing is that they have to show results. The good thing that Alex does in this book is that he actually shares real-world case studies that give you the other thing that I'm looking for, which is real world applicability. How does this really get proved out? Because theory is great, but you need to have examples, and Alex does a great job combining the theory with practical application here. And lastly, he makes it simple enough so it's great for anyone to follow to really get what this book promises, and it's a big promise—triple your sales and leads in under six months. Well, he absolutely shows you how to do that. I cannot recommend this book and Alex's services highly enough.

~Austin Netzley, author of *Make Money, Live Wealthy: 75 Successful Entrepreneurs Share the 10 Simple Steps to True Wealth*

I've been working with Alex for the past year, and his insight has been a big help to my business in both conversion rate and client retention. This book isn't merely theoretical; Alex uses case studies to illustrate how the system has been successfully applied to global businesses with positive, measurable results. The system provided in this book is actionable and can be applied to your business right now.

~Frank Salvatore, founder of *FlexLeads.com*

Ask questions & meet others on
Twitter, Instagram & Facebook using hashtag
#SmallBusinessBigMoney

Download Free Workbook, Videos and Course at:
SBBMO.com

Comments and Questions?
Email me: Alex@AlexDesigns.com

This book is dedicated to everyone who helped me make this book possible—those who gave feedback, those who contributed, and the awesome people I had the pleasure of interviewing on my podcast. This is for everyone who continuously supported all my endeavours. I couldn't have done it without you.

Your friend,
Alex

CONTENTS

FOREWORD:

I apologize if you try to hire Alex Harris and you find him really busy; that might be partially my fault. When we first met in 2004, he was a shy, young, somewhat experienced designer. In 1998 when my brother Jeffrey and I started our agency focused exclusively on helping companies increase their conversion rates, we were crazy pioneers. When Alex met us in 2004, the early adopters were few and far between. That makes Alex a veteran conversion rate optimization warrior, with the scars and victories commensurate with that.

We've brought Alex in to help on dozens of projects over the years; starting out with him freelancing while he held a full-time job at eDiets.com. He was a pleasure to work with. From the beginning, we recognized Alex's potential, his talent, and his willingness to learn. We've recommended his services to our clients over and over again. We still include Alex when projects are mission-critical because we know it guarantees any project's success. He is an invaluable business asset.

In fact, we do eat our own dog food. When launching the website for my new startup (IdealSpot.com), we engaged Alex for the design. Our website is converting like gangbusters. Learn from him or engage him; you deserve the same!

There are countless "designers" but only a small handful who purposely design for results. Designers who create websites to look pretty or win awards are often simply frustrated artists. Alex is a designer who focuses on conversion. He never lets his ego, current fads, or drama get in the way of a successful design.

I was flattered and enthusiastic to help when Alex asked me to write the foreword for this book. Alex has remained in the background for too long. He is way past due for the recognition he deserves.

You're going to get a lot out of this book. You'll get to know Alex and his disciplined approach better. Hopefully, you will follow his advice. If you're truly lucky, then you'll reach out to him and have him help you out.

I wish you happiness and the best of luck in all your endeavors.

Bryan Eisenberg, @TheGrok
Best-Selling Author & Keynote Speaker

PREFACE

Optimization is all about tweaking so you can squeeze more people through the funnel. For example, you have a thousand window shoppers, but only one buyer. If you can convince ten more people to buy, that's like a 10% increase, 10x the conversion rate.

~**Neil Patel,** Founder of QuickSprout and Co-founder of Kissmetrics and CrazyEgg

Over the past fifteen years, I have built more than 100 eCommerce sites and 1,000 landing pages and have executed over 7,000 different A/B tests. *Small Business Big Money Online* will give you direct, actionable advice and techniques that you can simply apply to your own process, developing your own system along the way. The process I've created to triple your sales and leads in under six months is called the Marketing Optimization System.

Conversion rate optimization is the method of creating an experience for a website or landing page visitor with the goal of increasing the percentage of visitors that convert into customers. Focusing on CRO introduced me to meet many great clients. In this book, I am going to highlight three of those clients in the case studies at the end of the book.

The process you will learn in this book is the Marketing Optimization System. The system includes the tools and techniques you will need to experiment quickly and effectively using CRO. Implementing your own version of this system will help you attain bigger results and grow your business faster. Adapting a well-planned marketing optimization system can help you *triple* your online sales in under six months.

Are you ready to triple your eCommerce sales and leads in under six months? If your website doesn't already have a Marketing Optimization System in place, then you have a huge opportunity for immediate growth.

This book will provide you with a step-by-step, detailed method to improve your conversion rates and generate more leads, as well as serve as a guide to use as you implement your own split testing and conversion rate optimization plan. Split testing is simply running two or more variations in your marketing creative to determine which is better. Start with the baseline control (your existing web page or creative elements) and implement a new version (the experiment) for comparison. You'll also learn how to think about your website differently. Not only does it need to look beautiful—it also needs to convert.

This book is filled with actionable advice. I will give you the tools to use, show you how to use those tools, and explain to you how you can get the best results from them.

AUTHOR'S NOTE

*Optimization encompasses finding the
right thing to improve and then improving
it on the most basic level.*
~Hiten Shah, Co-founder of Kissmetrics and CrazyEgg

I had the opportunity to meet Bryan and his brother Jeffrey at their Future Now Inc. office in Brooklyn, New York. They brought me in to understand more about what I was doing online as they had noticed I was doing a lot of landing pages, conversion funnels, and direct marketing for lead generation eCommerce companies.

I quickly realized that what Bryan and Jeffrey Eisenberg were doing was something I really wanted to be a part of. To do this, I needed to show them that I was reliable. If I could do that, then I knew that I could follow in the footsteps of their greatness. To establish my reliability, I began by offering my services for free, and I was subsequently able to produce some of the website designs they were looking for.

I was impressed by what they were doing with conversion optimization and persona marketing frameworks for conversion optimization. All of these innovative terms were new to me—prior to that, I had seen everything as just direct marketing. Then I learned about one of the simple concepts Bryan spoke about called the *Conversion Trinity*. Bryan told me about Dr. Ed Chi, a Xerox Palo Alto Researcher, who discovered that humans track information in a similar fashion to the way animals follow a scent. I applied this formula to every one of my new projects, and I immediately saw results.

INTRODUCTION

●●●●●●●●●●●●●●●●●●●●●●●●●

*Optimization is all about doing stuff
better and getting more results.
If you're selling stuff, optimization
will help you do it better. Optimization
is all about moving the needle.*

~Peep Laja, Founder of ConversionXL

Small business owners are frustrated. You've spent a lot of money on your web design, seemingly to no avail. You've hired a bunch of web developers and have someone running your pay-per-click marketing, but you're still not getting the ROI that you expect. And you know they need to act *now* before the competition gets closer. If not, you're going to be leaving a lot of money on the table. And as you pass through the different seasons of the year, you see that the results you seek are harder to come by. You understand your customers, but you don't talk directly to them. You see the numbers come in, and you look at the analytics, but you don't try to understand the data, so your web developers end up making *assumptions* about what the company should do.

To make matters worse, you, as the business owner, may have limited funds—and even more limited time. You may be either in startup or do-it-yourself mode. Right now, you're trying to do everything in a silo and getting inconsistent results. What you should really be doing is building out a well-thought-out optimization plan with a specialized team members. That's a completely different mindset—using your customer service to talk to your customers either through live chat, on the phone, or via Skype. It enables you to serve them in a much better capacity and get to know exactly what's going on in their minds—and then you can actually help them solve their problems.

In this book, you will learn a proven system to optimize your eCommerce website and increase your Internet profits. There are no magic tricks. There are no traffic generation gimmicks. The processes in this book will teach you how to make more money from your existing website traffic.

The framework I created to do this is called the Marketing Optimization System. It is a system based on knowing your customers, and serving them better because of what you've learned about it.

What is marketing? Marketing is simply moving goods from a producer to a consumer. It's the technique and the process of promoting, selling, and distributing those products and services.

Optimization, on the other hand, is making something as effective as it can possibly be. It is continuously improving your online business to make more profit. You're spending a lot of time and money on it, and that's exactly why you need to maximize your ROI.

Optimization comes in many different forms. Search engine optimization (SEO) works to improve your search engine rankings to drive more traffic to your site. Conversion rate optimization (CRO) involves improving your leads and sales to help make your websites more profitable. Other ways to achieve optimization include web design, web analytics, and utilization of social media.

I focus specifically on conversion rate optimization. Please note that not all aspects of this type of optimization may apply to you and the needs of your business. You may be using different tools and tactics to get the same results. Whatever your specific needs, however, implementing a marketing optimization process that allows you to predict the future and get compound results is necessary. Once you know it's working, you can replicate the winning results on other areas of your websites in a shorter amount of time and achieve an exponential growth factor.

> **ACTION STEP 1:**
> Go to SBBMO.com right now to download your free copy of the marketing optimization workbook. You want to have it in your hands so that you're prepared to take action right away. That's your first step. So go grab it now, and we'll get started!

MARKETING IN THE PAST

A lot of people get confused about the word "optimization" and think that they only need to optimize their sites for search engines. Really, you should be optimizing for revenue and profit. It doesn't matter how much traffic you drive to your website if you can't convert it.

~Theresa Baiocco, ConversionMax

I used to hate marketing.

From 2000 to 2011, I was the creative director of customer acquisition, an online eDiets website that sold personalized diet and fitness plans plus meal delivery. The marketing department would sell advertising on the website I prepared, and they would need us to create banner and e-mail campaigns at the very last minute. This happened every year at the same time—during the pre-holiday months. That meant spending the entire fall season creating marketing campaigns in preparation for the busiest season, which, in the diet industry, is after New Year's, after all the bingeing and merrymaking over the holidays. This is the time when people make their New Year resolutions—and the time when they are most motivated to start a new diet and exercise regimen.

Most companies today know about A/B testing. They know a little bit about conversion rate optimization, but unfortunately they're doing the slicing and dicing type of testing model and don't have a real strategy to help them optimize their initial process, getting them the results they need every single time. They're just making assumptions about what works. I learned—from my mistakes—that great marketing comes from truly understanding your visitors and then providing an experience that makes their lives better.

Let's look at the market out there—it's been reported that over 1.79 trillion dollars is left in abandoned eCommerce carts. Your unoptimized website experience may be contributing to this number. An eCommerce cart is "abandoned" when you visit an eCommerce site, see something you like, click on "add to cart", but never purchase the item.

For site owners, shopping cart abandonment is alarmingly on the rise. According to data shared with BI Intelligence by eCommerce data company Brilliance in 2013, as many as 74% of online shopping carts were abandoned by shoppers. That abandonment rate is up from 72% in 2012 and from 69% in 2011.

It will continue to increase as more customers shift to an online and mobile shopping experience. That's because people are only optimizing certain areas of their eCommerce templates. The classic eCommerce site has a homepage, a category page, and an item page, and it drives traffic to those core pages as well as to the checkout experience. Sadly, most people stop optimizing there. If they fail to optimize their checkout experience, and if their checkout experience is not appealing or enticing in any way, chances are you will be leaving a lot of money on the table.

ACTION STEP 2:
Have you done any conversion split testing in the
past? If yes, write down a few of your winning tests
and a few of your losing tests. Try to determine
if there was a good system in place.

Do you know your shopping cart abandonment rate?
If so, write it down and then come up with a new
goal for improvement.

MASTERING YOUR SYSTEM

*Optimization is just making something
better and aiming at the best that it can
possibly be and that the wonderful thing
about optimization is there's no finish line.
You'll never accomplish it. You can always
get better, and it's the striving in the
process in the journey that makes it
exciting and worthwhile.*

~**Rand Fishkin,** founder of Moz.com

In 2012, I realized that a lot of things on the web had really changed. There was a complete shift going on as people started to move away from SEO to focus on CRO. Remember, it doesn't matter how much traffic you direct to your website if it doesn't convert into sales.

I started to do more advanced testing, and I realized I was getting inconsistent results. I was following a lot of the same processes that I had learned many years before, but I didn't have an established system. I was doing slice and dice testing. I quickly realized that I had to educate myself. I needed to talk about conversion optimization and advanced digital marketing with like-minded people.

I realized I had to master the process of making more money for small online businesses. To do this, I needed to learn from the best in digital marketing. To connect with the best, I created a podcast, establishing myself as a thought leader. In 2013, I created the Marketing Optimization Podcast, interviewing the best in digital marketing, both in conversion optimization and web analytics. I asked some of my contacts—the top people in digital marketing—to be on my show.

And what I learned by interviewing over one hundred different digital marketing experts was that I was doing a lot of the same things they were doing. I just didn't have a system. I didn't have the right methodology, the kind they used to get results for their bigger clients. So I immediately began to create a framework for myself. I started to figure out what would work to get my eCommerce clients better results in a shorter amount of time.

And that's when I started to focus on mastering website conversions, determining what was working and what wasn't, and figuring out a framework I could start to use for my clients to get them better results—and also teach other people how to do it along the way. It was my "a-ha" moment—the moment I knew I was able to use a strategy, teach it to other people, and get my clients great results. This was the future, and the future looked bright.

ACTION STEP 3:
Who are the top thought leaders in your space? List twenty people who are doing amazing things with marketing in your business vertical.

Try to get as many of them as you can to meet with you. Invite them for coffee, hire them on Clarity.fm or set up a Skype call. Find out what tools they are using and how they're getting results from their marketing campaigns.

Find out how you can work together to help each other in your marketing efforts.

THE MARKETING OPTIMIZATION SYSTEM

Optimization is understanding your visitors.

~**Brian Massey,** founder of Conversion Sciences

The system I developed is called the Marketing Optimization system, the culmination of a process that begins with adopting a customer mindset, and then doing extensive research on your customers.

Its framework consists of three modules:

1. Customer Mindset – I will teach you to empathize with your customers by getting the right mindset. To get that mindset, you must consider the experience of the customer as the center of the universe and get to know your ideal customers. This involves studying the different types of personas that visit your website—ultimately leading them through the ideal click M.A.P. and seeing patterns of opportunity for growth.

2. Gathering Intelligence – Collecting data – in this case, qualitative and quantitative data - and analyzing them is at the heart of every step in the Marketing Optimization System. This module allows you to learn tips on how

you can use the data in a constructive way and apply them to the system in a way that best suits your needs.

3. Marketing Optimization System – Increase your sales and leads from your eCommerce website using this step-by-step system that I developed. Understand your customers and their problems, and create products that will solve their problems so you can improve your goals and get better results in a shorter amount of time.

Furthermore, the Marketing Optimization System is organized into three phases:

1. Strategic Evaluation – Break down your target market into your ideal customers during the first phase. You need to define your ideal customer, also known as an avatar. Having a clear understanding of your avatar allows you to identify their needs and speak to them in a language and voice that is familiar to them – the voice that they actually use.

2. 5-Step Process – The M.O. System is broken down into these five steps:

   a) Discovery. Involves quantitative and qualitative analysis and putting yourself in your customers' shoes to figure out exactly what is going on, allowing you to find areas of opportunity. You also get to learn how people use and interact with your websites.

   b) Hypothesis. After gathering your data, you need to create educated guesses to determine what needs to go on for conversion testing. After that, you will draw up a plan to help you get the biggest impact in the shortest amount of time.

   c) Execution. After you have gathered data and made educated guesses, you need to start getting things in motion. This phase is where you create all the tests and develop the creative for the differentiation variations in each experiment and set up the split testing software.

d) Review. Look back on your efforts and study your analytics to check if the new changes are helping your conversion rates. Remember that just because a split test wins doesn't mean you are making more money.

e) Scale. Now you are ready take your business to the next level, and make more money. After you have determined which tests are helping improve conversion rates, increase sales, and generate more leads, you can take what you have learned and apply it to other areas of your eCommerce store in order to sustain and further improve your positive results.

3. Bottom Line Growth – The key to growing your business quickly and effectively is in solid optimization. Remember that you need to ensure you are increasing your overall profit. This is where you reap the rewards from continuous iterative testing.

MARKETING OPTIMIZATION SYSTEM

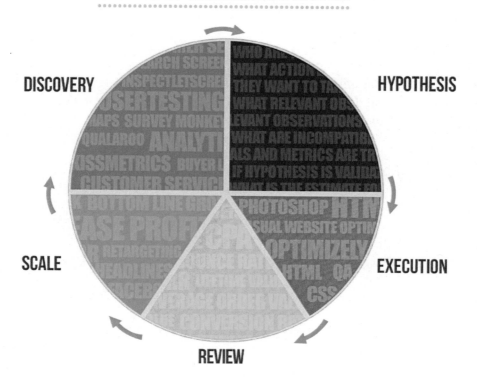

The rest of the book will be organized as follows. In chapter one, we will look at the first step of the process, the Customer Mindset. Chapter two will cover the Gathering Intelligence step. In Chapter 3, we will cover the Marketing Optimization System, including the three phases of the system: strategic evaluation, the five steps, and the bottom line growth plan.

In Part 2 of the book, I will present three case studies that show the system in action.

Here's a preview of the case studies:

- EnergyFirst.com
  Gerry Morton has been selling health and fitness supplements online since 1997. Using the Marketing Optimization System, we were able to increase the

amount of orders from the Whey Protein Page from an average of 130 sales per month to over 280 sales per month. It resulted in the overall the Cost Per Acquisition (CPA) going down by 50%, meaning we were spending less and generating a lot more profit. Plus the improvements we made to the lead generation strategy tripled the amount of new e-mail opt-ins we collected daily.

- MyTaxCoursesOnline.com
  Derek Woryn has been profiting from e-learning courses since 2002. I will show you how we took the winning elements of one site and applied them to several of their other websites and landing pages, increasing revenue and leads while decreasing cart abandonment rates. Using the Marketing Optimization System, we were able to increase MyTaxCoursesOnline.com's daily sales from 15 new daily customers to over 50 sales per day. On their MichiganBuildersLicense.com website, sales increased from 150 new customers to 450 sales per month.

- WiseChoiceMarket.com
  Simon Gorman is the founder of this eCommerce site using BigCommerce. They've been filling organic food delivery orders online since 2010. Using the Marketing Optimization System, we were able to dramatically impact the bottom line results for WiseChoiceMarket.com. From June through August of 2014, they averaged 450 orders per month, and then in January of 2015, they had over 1,350 sales. They also climbed from an average of 150 new customers per month in June through August to over 500 new customers per month in January. Also, after implementing the new lead generation strategy, we helped increase their new e-mail opt-ins from three subscribers per day to a daily average of over fifty new e-mail opt-ins.

ACTION STEP 4:

Make list of all of the previous achievements
your business has seen in the past.

List all the objectives you want to reach in the next six
months with your online business.

List all of the reasons your business might not achieve
the results you want in the next six months.

THE FUTURE OF MARKETING

●●●●●●●●●●●●●●●●●●●●●●●●●●●●●●●

Optimization is about increasing the efficiency of your marketing

~**Brendan Regan,** Conversion Optimization & Web Analytics Expert

Now I love marketing!

The online space has become a different world than it used to be. It used to be very simple to sell things online, but since we've moved into a more conscious usage of the Internet, people are more concerned about their security and their personal information being stolen. This explains the reluctance to input credit card information.

And that is exactly why we must optimize our websites to continuously understand what is working and what is not. If you don't optimize, measure, and iterate, you're probably not growing your business as fast as you possibly can. You're losing out on a lot of opportunities and wasting a lot of money in the process.

But what if you had an optimization plan? You have a sound process, a system you follow that helps you grow your business and take it to the next level. An optimization plan can help you spend the right amount of time, resources, and effort to test and make sound decisions to increase profit. This book will give you that plan.

I was recently quoted on Forbes.com as saying, "Every year we advance toward data-driven marketing. All design, advertising, and social media will be focused on driving measurable results using cutting-edge tracking and predictive analytics. Websites will focus more on optimizing conversion rates and increasing website traffic because it doesn't matter how much traffic you drive to your website if you're not converting that traffic into actual sales."

Small Business, Big Money Online is entirely focused on helping you make better decisions. You will be able to utilize the tools I recommend for your marketing and conversion rate optimization to get real, proven results—increasing conversions, generating more leads, and maximizing your return on investment.

ACTION STEP 5:

How has your industry changed over the last few years? Write down how marketing your business today is different than it was in the past.

Where do you think you might be losing money or wasting time on your marketing efforts?

Keeping other opportunities in mind, where can you make better decisions to increase your marketing campaigns results? Write down all areas.

PART ONE:
THE METHODOLOGY

CHAPTER - ONE
MODULE ONE: CUSTOMER MINDSET

● ●

I think about optimization – and more specifically, conversion – in terms of user experience and just about anything in a business. I really do think it's just a matter of making the things that you want to have happen, happen more often.

~**Clay Collins,** Co-Founder of LeadPages.net

To optimize successfully and efficiently, you must adopt the right mindset. The mindset you need is one of growth, not only from the perspective of being abundant and forward thinking, but also about your business as a whole.

During my years as a web designer, I never took a single marketing or business class. I learned everything through personal, hands-on experience and trial and error. And it was a *lot* easier to sell online from 2000 to 2006. We used to be able to simply put up a landing page and get a ton of leads and a very high conversion rate.

But today, it's a different story. We need to understand our business holistically, and we need to know our ideal customers. The right mindset will help you realize that consumers no longer buy the way they used to. We need to study the different types of personas coming to the website and know where they're going—consequently leading them through the ideal click M.A.P. This stands for the Marketing Along Path. This is the streamlined path you want the visitor to follow to become a customer.

You must execute goal-oriented strategies instead of relying on random marketing efforts. Come up with your own system—or use one that's already been created. This book will show you my system, and as you read through, you'll start to see a pattern of opportunity.

ACTION STEP 6:
Would you say you have an abundant or scarcity mindset? Please explain.

Do you truly know your customers?
Explain in as much detail as possible who you think your customers are.

BUYER LEGENDS

●●●●●●●●●●●●●●●●●●

Did you know that Jeff Bezos, in place of PowerPoint presentations in meetings, requires his execs to write six-page narrative memos?

~**Jeffrey Eisenberg,** Bryan Eisenberg, Anthony Garcia,
Buyer Legends: The Executive Storyteller's Guide

Buyer Legends is a process detailed in a book written by Bryan and Jeffrey Eisenberg. It is based on their signature framework Persuasion Architecture™, which you will learn about later. It becomes important as a blueprint to help us outline our customers' journey through our websites. We need to understand how people interact with our site and how they feel about our brands. Buyer Legends helps you deliver on the promise of your brand. This concept—creating narrative or story—is increasingly finding its way into the marketing world. The story that matters most is the story that takes place between the company and the customer. Without a story, all that's there is just data, more or less static. If you do not understand the context—the story of the interaction between the customer and the brand—you can interpret nothing.

But until now, the tools you've been given to understand the customers' actions have either been focused solely on the brand through the brand's story and branding or on the customer through personas. The tools have not focused on the decision-based marketing, shopping, buying, and experience that happens in the linked brand-and-customer experience. To understand this dynamic, you need to create the story. And this is where Buyer Legends comes in. Buyer Legends is a simple scenario narrative that helps identify the gap between the brand story and the brand experience. Buyer Legends ensures that all business decisions are made directly by the team responsible for the results and not indirectly through the creative, retail, customer service, legal, technology, or sales teams.

Using Buyer Legends is fundamentally different. It's hard work to think something completely through before doing it. There is a tremendous urge for us to take immediate action and start production, and this goes against that. You want to outline the story before you start creating any marketing material. That is how you begin to build the different personas for your ideal customers.

Once we have an understanding of the story from the buyers' points of view, we can then establish the ideal click M.A.P. for the customer. You want to map out your customer along a specific path. This is where we define our M.A.P. (Market Along Path). Ideally, you want to understand which pages each of your customer personas land on and create a M.A.P. for each of those different marketing experiences and campaigns. This is how you can get customers to convert with much less effort.

ACTION STEP 7:

Learn more about this process at BuyerLegends.com

List every possible reason a potential customer didn't buy at all or bought from a competitor.

List the reasons why a potential customer *did* buy a product from you and how it made them feel or the problem it solved for them.

Starting with the "Thank You" confirmation page and working backward, storyboard the customer journey in reverse chronology.

IDEAL CLICK M.A.P.

Optimization, in general, is interactive storytelling. You can keep people engaged, as long as you are telling stories that visitors want to be told. You are trying to give people what they are looking for. Determining the end goals can help you define how to tell the stories. It is beneficial because when you look at getting the most of out the experience that you are creating in the story. You end up looking at the bigger picture.

~**Tommy Walker,** Marketing at Shopify

To have successful marketing campaigns, you need to learn from experience. You'll need to use the insight you've gained over the years of running your business. As you gain this intellect and intuition, it will become your mindset. Your mind will shift from thinking that you need to drive more traffic or spend more money on advertising to realizing that you should instead be trying to increase the number of people who spend money with you. Instead of driving traffic, we are now going to focus on improving conversions. We need to ask ourselves, *what happens post click?* After potential clients or customers arrive at your website, how can you lead them through a specific and ideal click map that will get them from start to finish?

M.A.P. stands for marketing along a specific path. Creating your ideal M.A.P. will lead your target audiences through a specific set of pages, defining their journey. Here's a definitive example of a M.A.P. for eCommerce. An individual types a keyword into Google then clicks on a pay-per-click advertising campaign. This then leads them to a landing page. The landing page could be a custom web page, a category page, a specific product detail page, or even your homepage. I don't recommend sending paid advertising to your homepage, however. The landing page should have one focus that directly helps the visitor with the problem (query) they were searching for in Google. The solution to that problem is the goal for that instance of the M.A.P. That conversion goal could be a lead, a sale, or just a click.

In eCommerce, when a customer lands on a product category page, they are more likely to click an item, and from that item, they will be directed to a product detail page. This is the page where they can add something to a cart. Once they click "add to cart", they are then sent to a shopping cart page where they can view items in their shopping cart basket and then click to check out. As they go through the checkout process, they're eventually taken to a thank you or confirmation page.

This is the ideal M.A.P. for an eCommerce. You want to create a M.A.P. specific to your particular marketing experience while keeping the customer's best interests a priority.

ACTION STEP 8:
Using the storyboard you created for your customer journey, outline a flow chart of your ideal M.A.P. On this flow chart, list the goals for each page. Describe what you want the visitor to accomplish in each section.

You should have an ideal M.A.P. for each of your marketing campaigns. Create one for your mobile traffic, for your social media visitors, and for your paid advertising.

PERSUASION ARCHITECTURE

*It was not about winning awards;
it was about getting results*
~**Bryan Eisenberg,** Best-Selling Author & Keynote Speaker

You need to think of your customer as the center of the universe. For each type of customer, you want to understand the different types of personas that visit your websites. A persona is a particular type of individual who is visiting your websites. It is more than just average demographics—personas also take into account the overall goal of the individual, how they use your websites, and the customer's voice.

Persuasion Architecture™ is the framework that Bryan Eisenberg and his brother Jeffrey created to persuade customers when they ignore marketing. Persuasion Architecture™ begins with the premise that the buying decision process and the sales process must work in tandem. The solution for dramatically improving conversion rates does not lie in helping businesses "sell better." It lies in helping businesses marry the sales process to their audience's buying decision processes—in essence, the business must provide a structure that helps the prospect "buy better."

For you to achieve your goals, your visitors must first achieve their goals. Only when you help your audience buy better will you be able to sell better.

The Phases of Persuasion Architecture™:
Persuasion Architecture has six phases. The process begins with Uncovery, continues with Wireframing, Storyboarding, and Prototyping, and then enters the actual coding phase in Development. The final phase provides for testing, measuring, and optimization, an ongoing process that ensures your

management decisions are always based on solid information. The following pages describe each phase of Persuasion

Architecture in more depth.

1. **Uncovery**
   Uncovering the buyer personas through narratives

2. **Wireframing**
   Wireframing out every single step and persona along the entire journey

3. **Storyboarding**
   Storyboarding the creative

4. **Protoyping**
   Prototyping the design and functionality

5. **Development**
   Developing the final experience

6. **Optimizing**
   Optimization and testing measurement

Uncovery

The goals of Uncovery are to match the value of your business to what matters most to the customer. To better understand the customer, you'll start to create customer "personas," which are almost like narrative avatars of your customers. You will develop stories of your customers as they are walking through their buying process and encountering your business. What do they see? What key words or phrases in your value proposition attract them? How do their needs, wants and desires fit with your business objectives? Uncovery, the first step toward designing and developing effective persuasion architecture, follows a logical four-step process:

- Step 1. Analyze your business, from your business model and products to customers and competitors.

- Step 2. Identify your business goals and objectives and your key performance indicators.
- Step 3. Develop your customer personas.
- Step 4. Develop the scenarios for those personas.

Wireframing

Wireframing is a detailed "mapping" of your sales process for the personas' buying process. In other words, you "follow" them as they navigate through your website, taking into account any possible path that they might take. Through the links in your wireframe, you will see the site from the perspective of the customer, and this will generate useful feedback at a time when changes are easy.

Storyboarding

This phase of Persuasion Architecture focuses on persuasive content, layout and design. If the wireframe is the "what" of Persuasion Architecture, the storyboard is the "how." The goal here is to flesh out the wireframe, filling in the words and the graphics.

Start with the persuasive copy: everything that has to be written. You already had some barebones text in the wireframe. Now focus on making that text persuasive.

Next, you create a first mockup of the storyboard. You'll be considering different elements, ranging from branding and navigation to detailed issues such as header graphics and even copyrights and privacy notices.

The next step is to move toward the actual design of the site. Start in grayscale: you want to see how the structure and words work with the emotional impact of color. Once you have your full design in grayscale, add the color. A color scheme is important for a variety of reasons, including the emotional feel of your site and cohesiveness of the different pages.

The final step is your image into an HTML document, with the usual web considerations (e.g., choosing fonts that can be read easily, using cascading sheets for simplicity, and so on).

Prototyping:

The next phase of Persuasion Architecture is to create a prototype, just as architects create full models of their final buildings. Your prototype will be an actual operational model of your site. Make all the changes you can think of now — it's still easy and cheap.

Development:

This final phase should be the easiest because all of the decisions have been made in the previous phases. The only function now is to program — or more accurately, have your developers create the programming — to transform what you've planned and decided into reality.

Optimization:
You now have a finished product, and it's time for the final phase testing and measuring. You will now learn through monitoring your Web analytics whether your decisions in the previous phases meet your expectations and objectives. And if they don't, you'll have to make some changes.

This book is about optimization — about working with the finished product until you are fully satisfied that you are getting the best results from every page.

Applying Persuasion Architecture to web marketing makes everything measurable (although not all data yield useful information!). The result is a Marketing Optimization 5-Step process that enables continuous improvement.

ACTION STEP 9:
List three different personas that fit
your ideal customer.

> See how this formula applies to your website,
> landing pages and advertisements.
>
> These answers do not need to be perfect or correct.
> You just want to gather your ideas on paper.

BUYER MODALITIES
● ●

*Credibility sets the stage. Logic leads
to conclusion. Emotion leads to action.
Strategically balancing all three
persuades conversion.*
~**Angie Schottmuller,** Inbound Marketing Advisor

Another great concept for understanding your customers' purchasing patterns is called Buyer Modalities. The expert on this subject is Angie Schottmuller, a great speaker on how to apply website psychology to conversion rate optimization. She discusses specific methods to use in order to understand the distinct modalities of the buyers who visit your websites. People think in different ways, and their different personalities determine the feelings they get when visiting your pages. There's a huge difference between buyers who purchase based on logic versus those who make decisions based on emotion.

There are four types of buyer-buying modalities—four ways that buyers interact with and think about your site. The four modalities are *competitive, spontaneous, methodical,* and *humanistic.* Competitive and spontaneous buyers are fast and have quick reactions while methodical and humanistic buyers are slow and somewhat unstructured.

Those comprising the competitive modality are fast, but they make structured and logic-based decisions. They ask *"What makes your solution the best?"* because *they* want to be the best. Spontaneous buyers are all about quick, unstructured, and emotion-based decisions. *Why should I choose you, right now? What are you going to do for me immediately?*

In contrast, there are the two slower buyer modalities. Methodical buyers make structured and logic-based decisions—just like the competitive group—but they take their time. They often want to know *how* your process or solution works. The humanistic bunch are also slow in making a decision, but they do it in a more unstructured and emotional way. They ask, *"Who uses your solution for my problem?"* and *"How does it relate to the individuals at hand?"*

Knowing these four buyer modalities will help you understand precisely who is visiting your site and how you need to approach them and talk to them. You have to shift your mindset and try to understand your websites in a completely different way. This is a strong basis for understanding the framework that will work for you and your business.

Buyer modalities may be important to you, web analytics may be important to you, and the right qualitative data may be important to you. I'm going to show you what has proven to work for *me*, but you need to try to figure out the right system for *you*—in your own scenario, for the people visiting your websites, and for your experience.

BUYER MODALITIES CHECKLIST

COMPETITIVE
Bottom line UVP , "Best" evidence, Learn/achieve challenges ✔

SPONTANEOUS
Personalization, Guarantee, Time-savers/Tools, Hot trends/Urgency ✔

METHODICAL
Process Steps, Factual details, Timing expectations ✔

HUMANISTIC
People/Others-focused, People photos, Stories & Reviews ✔

Eisenberg, Bryan. Eisenberg, Jeffrey. David, Lisa T. 2006. Persuasive Online Copywriting.

ACTION STEP 10:
What type of buyer do you think frequents
your site the most? How do you think you might
best attract this kind of buyer?

List the buyer modalities and describe how each
type may react to your websites content.

Brainstorm ideas on how you could change
your websites to appeal to each different buyer
modality. Write those ideas down.

CHAPTER - TWO
MODULE TWO: GATHERING INTELLIGENCE

* * *

Many people, particularly in the small business community, think conversion rate optimization is all about driving as much traffic as possible. Try to optimize your website so it converts more of your visitors that you're already receiving into sales or leads without buying additional levels of traffic.

~**Rich Page,** author of Web Optimization an Hour a Day

At every step in the Marketing Optimization System, we collect and analyze data in two different ways—qualitatively and quantitatively. Analyzing qualitatively helps you to understand exactly who visits your websites and know why they should be buying products from your online store. Quantitative data is all about numbers and metrics. It is the analytics and the goals that are calculated from your marketing results.

I highly recommend that you test *all* of the concepts listed in this book. Conversion optimization is that testing process and the continuous improvements you implement as a result to make your websites more profitable.

In the next few chapters, we will discuss specific tools and goals that will enable you to test and track the success of your marketing efforts. Then we'll break down how to analyze the qualitative insight and quantitative data to gain actionable information.

It's one thing to gather all this insight, but the difficult part is using it in a constructive way that will result in higher sales and leads. Here, I will share tips to help you with each of the different tools. You can then apply them to our system in a way that best suits your needs.

Once you determine the things that help your websites to make more money or increase your conversion rates, you can scale those things up to increase your bottom line.

ACTION STEP 11:
Which tools are you currently using on your
websites to collect qualitative insight?

Which tools are you currently using on your
websites to collect quantitative insight?

Which goals are you currently tracking
for your websites?

TOOLS AND GOALS

*You must be consistently working
to improve results.*

~Hunter Boyle, Content Marketer & Optimization Pro

Now it's time to create the right tool kit for *your* Marketing Optimization System. In this section, I'll talk about some of the different technologies you may want to use, and we'll discuss these tools in the upcoming case studies as well. What goes into the ideal tool kit for your marketing optimization plan?

I recommend a tool kit using:

- Google Analytics to measure your data

- HotJar for exit polls, heatmaps, scrolling data, and mouse tracking

- Visual Website Optimizer or Optimizely for split testing

- SurveyMonkey to gather feedback in survey format

- UserTesting to watch people go through your web pages

- Unbounce to create landing pages for paid advertising and lead generation landing pages

- LeadPages to create e-mail opt-in landing pages for Facebook Ads

- ECommerce Dashboard (WordPress, Shopify, Bigcommerce, Magento, etc.)

Once you've stocked your tool kit, the next step is to determine your goals. You want to identify both your quantifiable goals and your qualitative goals. For example, for a blog, one of your goals might be to increase shares and comments on your content. In a service-based business, your goal may be to collect leads.

In eCommerce, you'll have many different kinds of goals—increasing your average order value, creating more profit, and increasing your conversion rates from your marketing campaigns to boost your overall bottom line. You also want to optimize to improve the opt-ins and build your e-mail list. You want to improve your returning customer revenue and increase your leads for mobile. You also want to decrease the bounce rate of your top landing page. This, in return, will also decrease the time it takes a new customer to make a first purchase.

Decreasing the time to order is an important goal for eCommerce. To do this, you need to figure out works best for you. To do that, start by creating what we call the 80-20. Most eCommerce sites make 80% of their revenue off of 20% of their inventory. Make sure that you know what that 20% is—and promote those products on your site. That way, you can get a large number of people to purchase more in a shorter period of time.

Once you understand your data and know what your goals are, then you can proceed to testing and analysis. Breaking the overall conversion into a series of steps will help you identify where all of this should lead, directing you through a funnel to your ultimate end goal. Looking at the big picture will enable you to look at your data—customer referrals, high traffic bounce rate pages, high-traffic/low bounce rate pages, specific high countries—in a different way. Knowing where to start depends both on your data and your knowledge of where you can achieve the biggest gains with the least amount of effort. You must understand how much time and traffic it'll take you to achieve statistical significance. In nonmathematical jargon, statistical significance tells you something about the degree to which your results are "true" and representative of your testing audience. You want to ensure that you run your tests for at least a hundred conversions on each variation, but the exact number might be unique to your own website.

The next step is to research to gather as much data—both quantitative and qualitative—as possible before starting the marketing optimization process. Gathering data is the most time-consuming part of the process because we then need to analyze that data to use it in an accurate way.

ACTION STEP 12:
Which new tools do you plan to use on your websites to collect qualitative insight?

Which new tools do you plan on using for your websites to collect quantitative insight?

Which products are making up 80% of the revenue (sales) on your websites? List all your best sellers and then list the average monthly sales for each of those products.

QUALITATIVE INSIGHT

●●●●●●●●●●●●●●●●●●●●●●●

Optimization is, from a psychological angle, is figuring out how best to meet the goals and the motivations of your customers, of your own people. It's not just about optimizing website elements—copy, content, and such—to get certain behaviors, it's also optimizing the psychological experience in getting people. What is some of that implicit motivation, explicit motivations, how can you encourage them to connect with you on a deeper level around common values? All of these things have to be considered when you're creating any kind of experience online.

~**Nathalie Nahai,** The Web Psychologist

Using qualitative insight can seem daunting, and it does take a lot of time. But it's the most important part of the entire Marketing Optimization System. In fact, the tasks that are usually the toughest to scale are the ones that make the biggest difference. For example, getting on the phone with visitors to your site who abandoned your shopping cart can take a lot of time and effort, yet talking directly to these visitors is exactly where the biggest untapped opportunities lie.

It is here where you will learn what's going on in your potential customer's mind. You don't ever want to make assumptions about what your visitors want. You need to ask them, give surveys, or listen to customer service calls to understand why they are—or are not—purchasing products from your store. Once you have clearly defined the problems they're having and learn what is missing from your site, you can then create specific solutions. As you know more about what is going on in your customers' minds, you can optimize your eCommerce site to display the copywriting, benefits, and unique value they're looking for on your eCommerce website.

The best copywriting will be taken directly from the customers, using language they understand, and addressing their problems—therefore making their lives better.

I have found that most people do not buy on logic, they buy on emotion. There is an emotional trigger in their lives that makes them head to Google and search for a solution to their problem. After they get there, it may take a few touch points with your brand to make them return and purchase. Use e-mail and retargeting marketing campaigns to keep your brand at the top of your potential customer's mind. A retargeting marketing campaign is when advertisements from a site you visit begin to appear on other websites that you visit. Potential customers will start comparing your brand directly to whomever they think their competitors are. Considering this, you can see that it's very important to understand how your customer feels about your competitors so that you can clearly differentiate yourself.

For example, an Internet user will visit Google and search for a particular type of product or for a solution to a problem they have. You want to be there to solve their problem. You want to understand what they're looking for and where they may go to find it. Your ads need to address the specific problem. And beyond that initial step, your landing page needs to present solutions that will make their lives better. That's what qualitative data is all about—building customer profiles, defining personas, and creating ideal click M.A.P.s, removing any unnecessary friction or difficulty.

You also want to know all of the keywords potential buyers are looking for. Not only the keywords they're typing into their search, but also those that are actually driving the most profit to your site. What is your customer's intent, and what keywords are actually driving the most conversions and leads?

So how do we figure this out? Understanding qualitative data can be difficult, but there are many different tools you can use to "read" your potential customer's mind. This is known as learning the *voice* of the customer.

UserTesting

One of the tools I use in every project is UserTesting. What other brands are they clicking on? What is their user experience going to be? How are people actually finding your site? UserTesting helps answer these questions. It's a pen that enables you connect the dots and determine how people are using your site. It will also help you see why people are or are not completing the checkout process.

You will also want to use UserTesting to analyze your competitors. Make a list of the sites you think are your main competitors and use the same tool to watch people go through those sites. This will help you identify what customers like or dislike about other sites, and you can use this data to compare to your own site. You'll be able to define your customer profile better and speak to individuals with direct marketing messages aimed at solving their specific problems.

Here are some tips for questions to ask when setting up UserTesting:
I RECOMMEND USING SCREENERS TO GET QUALITY PEOPLE IN YOUR TESTS.

Question 1 - First Impressions

View homepage (or landing page) and talk about the site. What can you do here? What do they sell? Do you trust this company? Do they look reliable? Why or why not?

Question 2 - Checkout Process

Find the [PRODUCT] you want and quickly go through the process of buying it—all the way to the end of the checkout process. If this hadn't been a test, would you have made a purchase? Why or why not? Was the order process missing anything?

Question 3 - Competitive Analysis

Who do you think are the competitors of this site? Go to Google and search for a similar product. Try to order it from a competitor. Which experience did you prefer, and why? Identify what specifically was better or worse about each site?

Question 4 - Returns, Privacy, and Trust

Imagine that you need to return your purchase and get your money back. How would you do that? Do you trust that this site would give you a refund?

Question 5 - Magic Wand

If you had a magic wand, how would you improve DOMAINNAME.com?

SurveyMonkey

SurveyMonkey is the next tool that we use on every project. It's an easy way to create and publish online surveys in minutes and then view the results graphically and in real time. SurveyMonkey provides free (up to 100 responses) online questionnaire and survey tools that can help generate qualitative insight.

You want to use open-ended questions so people can tell you as much as possible about their experience with your business, but the survey should be relatively short. I recommend a feedback form with three to five questions and an optional sixth question in which the user can enter their contact information. If a visitor reports a bug or any issues they had with your website, and they leave their e-mail address, you should contact that person personally—either on the phone or via Skype–to learn more about the issue and brainstorm ways to fix it.

The goal of the survey is to get 100 responses. To achieve this, you are going to have to promote the survey in a few different ways. Add it to your conversion thank you page, add a feedback link to your header and footer navigation, and include the survey link in the signature of all your customer service e-mails. Ask your Facebook fans to complete it and promote it in your e-mail newsletters. Surveys will encourage your customers by showing them that you care and want to make their shopping experience even better.

Here is an example of a great three to five question feedback form using SurveyMonkey.

Question 1 – How long have you been a customer of DOMAINNAME.com?
Use radio buttons to display the answers for people to click.
Example:
5+ Years
1-5 Years
Less than 1 Year
Haven't Purchased Yet

Question 2 – How did you learn about DOMAINNAME.com?
Use radio buttons to display the answers for people to click.
Example:
Friend or family recommendation
Doctor recommendation
Web Search
Other (please specify)

Question 3 – What is your biggest challenge in life right now?
Show a comment box that allows the user to type a long form message with their answers.

Question 4 – What other websites or store do you purchase from aside from DOMAINNAME.com?
Show a comment box that allows the user to type a long form message with their answers.

Question 5 – How can we improve DOMAINNAME.com?
If you had a magic wand, how would you improve DOMAINNAME.com?

Question 6 - (Optional) Please enter your contact information:
Name
E-mail Address
Phone Number

HotJar

Another great tool we highly recommend is HotJar. HotJar records videos of your visitors as they use your site, allowing you to see everything they do—every mouse movement, scroll, click, and form interaction. It's free for up to a certain amount of sessions, but HotJar is a must for every website you own.

To get the most out of using a tool like HotJar, I recommend a daily inspection of the data. At first, you can ignore all the session recordings that are less than three pages in length. Just watch the session recordings with the longest lengths. While viewing them, you will see how the visitor is browsing your website—where they go, what they're clicking on, and why they are or are not converting to a sale or lead. It's like getting a live quality assurance test on your customer's journey through your website. If the visitor browses a few pages then moves on to add something to the cart, you can see the M.A.P. that they chose to take.

For example, when a customer visits a category-specific page coming from Google, HotJar will show you where their mouse moves, how far they scroll, and what they click on. If the visitor seems to be interested in the product, they will click on "add to cart" and then go to the shopping cart. Here, you will see how far they get into the checkout experience. If they don't check out, it might prompt you to determine that the shopping cart user interface—or even the price—is causing them to abandon. This is paramount in helping us form a hypothesis of where we should begin to optimize. This process can be done for any page on your website, and it provides priceless information.

HEATMAPS / MOUSE TRACKING

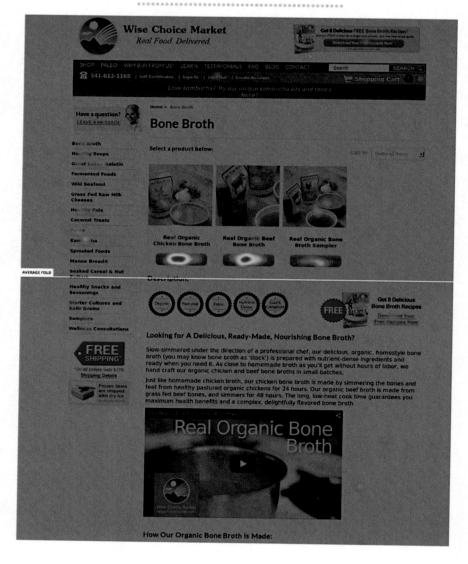

Qualaroo

Another great qualitative tool is Qualaroo. Qualaroo makes it possible to use intelligent pop-up surveys depending on different variables. For example, you can trigger a survey to a visitor based on the amount of time on page, pages visited, number of site visits, referring source, or any internal data. These interactions can be used to gather insights about visitors, address their unique needs in real time, and ultimately turn them into valuable customers.

The best place to use Qualaroo is on your cart or checkout page. A survey will pop up if the customers move their mouse toward the "back" button. In the survey, we try to determine why they aren't checking out. We want to know their intent and why they may not be buying. We also use Qualaroo on the conversion thank you page after a purchase and ask, "What made you purchase from us today?" Surveys can help you understand why people are *not* taking the action you want as well as why people *are* taking the action you want. There's no better time to engage with your actual customers than after they actually connect with you and your site in some way— whether it be on the e-mail opt-in thank you page or after the purchase confirmation.

Now that you've followed these suggestions and have your ideal customer profile, one of the key tips I can give you is to reach out to as many customers and as many people who didn't convert as possible. You want to get people on the phone—understand exactly how they found you, what their intent was before finding you, and why they did or did not convert. Talk to all of your direct ideal customers and understand exactly what their real problems are. The more you talk to people, the more you will understand your "audience" and know exactly what problems that they have, what they want and need, and how you can help serve them better in the future. The more research you do, the better off you will be.

So you may be asking, *why do all this?* Well, you do it because it really does help you to better define the personas visiting your site. Making guesses and assumptions doesn't help you achieve or improve, and it certainly doesn't help your potential customers find what they're searching for. This is so much more important than spending money on advertising. All of this qualitative data comes into play with predictive analysis. If you're able to connect the dots properly, you can almost always predict how your advertising campaigns are going to work. This insight is the secret to increasing your sales and leads in the next six months.

ACTION STEP 13:

Try UserTesting.com on your websites or landing page. Choose the Ideal M.A.P. that correlates directly with the top revenue generating products. Then set up UserTesting.com to watch visitors go through the websites experience.

Try SurveyMonkey.com and set up a feedback form. Aim to get at least 100 responses to this survey.

Set up HotJar.com and add the code to your websites. Make a practice of reviewing the heatmaps and mouse tracking one to two times a week.

QUANTITATIVE DATA

Optimization is about more than percentage points. It's about moving from a business to a brand. Every element of your marketing experiences has the potential to positively influence and delight your future customers. Don't design to acquire customers, design to acquire your ideal customer. Only then are you optimizing experiences targeted at lifetime value as opposed to conversion rate.

~**Oli Gardner,** Cofounder of Unbounce

I'm not an analyst, but I know the right places to look for the right data.

Quantitative data is all about the numbers, but finding the right data can often seem like looking for a needle in a haystack. The majority of people use Google Analytics, but there are also tools like KISSmetrics, Mixpanel, and Heap Analytics. These are more advanced analytics platforms that may or may not work for your business.

But to get started, let's look at how to analyze our website stats using Google Analytics. I've struggled with this myself in the past but have figured out a reliable process to get the best information from this tool. You will use the data you gather to make better decisions and get a bigger impact from your marketing efforts.

Quantitative data—it's all about numbers, visits, traffic, bounce rates, time on site, social shares, visits to your about page, and total conversions. Most sites are built upon the 80/20 rule. You will use Google Analytics to figure out which 20% of your pages are making up 80% of your traffic. To do this, visit your

Google Analytics dashboard, click Behavior, then Site Content, and then Landing Pages. These are the pages that visitors are going to directly. You may see that your homepage is the top traffic landing page, but you should locate five other top pages, categories, or product detail pages. View the topic traffic landing pages and the top sessions to determine where you can start optimizing on a page-by-page basis.

If you have eCommerce tracking and conversion goals set up, then you should be able to organize your top traffic pages by revenue. Google Analytics also shows the bounce rate for each of your top traffic pages. The bounce rate represents the percentage of visitors who enter the site and "bounce" (leave the site) rather than continuing to view other pages within the same site. You should make a note of all of the pages with a bounce rate higher than 55%. One of your goals should be to reduce the bounce rate of each of these pages to below this percentage.

Some tips to reduce bounce rate include:

- Determine where the referral traffic is coming from on each of these pages and possibly remove links that are causing you to receive unqualified traffic.

- Have quality links to other areas of your website above the screen fold.

- Do not have external links (links that point to other domains) above the screen fold.

- Show your best selling items with call-to-action buttons above the fold.

- Don't assume the visitor knows what to do next. *Tell them*. Instruct them to click a product, fill out a form, or search for another product.

- Find other ways to keep visitors on your website. For example, add videos, quizzes, and related blog posts that require visitor interaction to your domain.

So now you have additional data—you know the pages with the highest bounce rates, those with the most traffic, and also those with the most revenue. It's very common in eCommerce for a few of your pages to be receiving just as much traffic as the homepage, and that's because you should not be sending your paid marketing campaigns to the homepage. Through research and testing, I have already determined that sending paid per click (PPC) advertising to a homepage is a complete waste of money. Your PPC ads should drive visitors to category, product, or custom landing pages. This will help create an isolated experience to maximize your return on investment.

Google Analytics will help you identify the five major pages on which to start your conversion testing. The next step is to use a revenue tracking software like Visual Website Optimizer (VWO). You are not starting a real test just yet—you just want to get revenue tracking and conversion tracking with heatmaps working properly on those particular pages. Heatmaps show what people are clicking on, and using the heatmaps in VWO will help you determine exactly where to test. VWO also gives you the amount of revenue each of the pages is generating. You want to determine how many days it takes to reach 100 sales or 250 leads. This will determine the baseline control conversion rate, revenue amount, and click rate for each of the top pages in our Marketing Optimization System.

After using VWO, you have a quantitative profile of the top traffic pages, the top pages by revenue, and the top pages by bounce rate. This creates a hypothesis for our quick-win process. You've just learned where to start testing, some options to test, and how long it will take to see results. You optimize the section that is getting the most clicks, and if you're able to increase the clicks or the conversion just from that one spot on that one page, more than likely you're going to have a *huge* win.

Let's take a look at an example of how to find a quick win for your eCommerce website. Let's say you're selling jewelry. The rings category page has a 50% bounce rate. The diamonds category page has an 80% bounce rate, but they both have about the same amount of traffic and the same amount of revenue. You'd start optimizing at the diamond page section. Maybe halfway down the page, there's a particular opt-in, or a bestselling item, or a featured item, or an item under $100. You learn that the majority of people are clicking there—so now you know that you need to spend time optimizing the calls-to-action, the headlines, and whatever else is right there in that particular section. It's a top traffic page, it has a high bounce rate, it has a lot of opportunity to increase their revenue, and you now know exactly where on the page now to test.

You've used only *one* piece of data from Google Analytics, applied Visual Website Optimizer to it to track revenue and heatmaps, and now you're able to build out your first hypothesis. This is exactly the kind of thing that you can do on a continuous basis across every area of your eCommerce store. We get this granular on creating micro-goals based on our quantitative data. Micro-goals are the actions that lead up to the ultimate conversion goal, the sale. Then you apply a quantitative analysis of what you learned in order to make better decisions for that test. Since the majority of people are spending their time on that particular part of that particular page, that's where you are going to direct your focus to make the most money.

If you are doing PPC, you also want to determine the keywords people are searching for before they even start their Google query. You can go into Google AdWords and do keyword search terms by match type and learn the conversion and the revenue for each keyword. Not only do you know "by page" now, but you also know which keywords are converting and which are wasting your money. Now you can concentrate your time on the things that are already winning for you and begin to remove all of the negative keywords that aren't working. Decreasing your cost per acquisition (CPA) while simultaneously improving your quality score on your landing page results in improving your conversion rate on a per keyword basis.

Win, win, win. That's the key to setting up your Marketing Optimization System to triple your sales and leads in under six months.

ACTION STEP 14:

Go to Google Analytics and view your Top Traffic Landing Pages. Find the pages receiving the majority of your traffic. List the five pages (not including your homepage) that are receiving the most traffic.

Determine the landing pages that have high bounce rates (higher than 55%). Look at each of these pages and list five ideas to reduce the bounce rate on each of those pages.

Set up Visual Website Optimizer on each of these five pages and determine the amount of revenue that each page generates over a period of two to four weeks or a total amount of 200 conversions, whichever comes first. Record the information for each of the pages on the lines below.

CHAPTER - THREE
MODULE THREE: MARKETING OPTIMIZATION SYSTEM

Let's bring everything together into a more advanced process that I call the Marketing Optimization System. It's a five-step process to increase profit from the existing traffic of your eCommerce website. You can use what I've learned to help you make better decisions and get bigger results. There are many other tools that can be used and things that can be done, but I have included only the essential steps that I believe are needed in *every* system.

Creating the right system for you is all about gathering the qualitative and quantitative data and using that insight to obtain bigger impacts from our tests. It doesn't matter how much testing you do or how easy the testing is—*if you're not testing the right things, then you're not getting the best results possible.*

Marketing optimization takes into account web design, marketing in general, web development, web analytics, and the customers who visit your websites. Do you understand the voice of the customers who are visiting your websites? Who's your target audience? What are their pains, and what are the problems they're dealing with before they actually arrive? What queries are they entering into Google before arriving at your landing pages? These are some of the things I'll be showing you—the importance of knowing who visits your site, where they go, what they do, and what you should do with that information.

ACTION STEP 15:

Now is the time to set your objectives at the highest level. List some of the big goals you want to accomplish by creating a system.

Where do you want to take your online business? In your mind, what dream achievements would make your business an ultimate success?

What websites do you think are accomplishing your goals? List five websites that you think are achieving the type of web design and the success that you want for your website.

PHASE 1 - STRATEGIC EVALUATION

Your first step is to break down your target market into your ideal customers. Your ideal customer is also known as an *avatar*. Defining your customer avatar is critical. You see, most companies and retailers are not meeting their customers' needs. You need to ensure that you have a clear understanding of your customers' needs and are targeting the right audience so that you can speak to them in a language they're familiar with. The voice or language you want to use is *their* voice.

Here is where you will use the customer's mindset —it will be the foundation for the personas that are more likely to buy from your online store. You want to understand the average demographics of your ideal customers—where they live, their age range, if they have children, average household income, and where they shop online. You also want to understand the lifestyle factors of your visitors. What are their hobbies and interests? How do their emotional states affect their buying modes? In addition, you can use Google Analytics to segment the visitors based on the different browsers they're using to view your website. How many visitors are using the desktop version versus a mobile or a tablet?

Each time you publish content on your site, you need to keep your target audience in mind.

ACTION STEP 16:

Think about your current customer base. Write a description of who you think your customers are and what you think their needs are.

Write down the demographics of your ideal customers.

Next, think about your ideal customer base. Describe them and brainstorm what you might need to do to attract them. Is it different from what you're currently doing?

PHASE 2 – 5-STEP PROCESS

The key to a successful strategy is iterating quickly and never ceasing in the quest for improvement. Then we need to validate each hypothesis using split testing. Here is where I will walk you through the 5-Step Process of the Marketing Optimization System.

Start with qualitative insight, and understand that *why*. What is actually going on in your customers' minds? Do they like your products? How can you address their concerns when they first arrive at your /product pages? If they don't purchase, can you determine what influenced that decision?

Then, create different personas for people. Build these personas to create ideal click M.A.P.s for each visitor. Learn the pains, problems, and desires of each of your ideal customers. Talk to your visitors as much as you possibly can. They will let you in on their secrets about your website. This will enable you to stop making assumptions about what you think your customers want.

Next, bring in the quantitative data to see where your customers are actually going on your site. This is all based on the 80/20 rule. You make 80% of your traffic from 20% of your pages. You break it all up into your most trafficked pages, your most trafficked pages by revenue, your highest bounce rate pages, and then your top AdWords by conversion rate.

After that, you want to separate your personas based on the research you've gathered. For example, you want to know things like:

- How many people are using your site on an old computer?
- How many visitors are browsing within a mobile experience?
- How are people really seeing your websites?
- Which Internet browsers are your customers using the most?

Don't assume your visitors are using the latest computer technology. Know their favorite browsers—Safari? Chrome? Internet Explorer? If you have a lot of people using old IE browsers, it could mean they're in schools or government agencies, and that will define your demographic. It's a very important part of building your persona.

You may also want to document your business goals and see what is most important to the business stakeholders. Then can prioritize the ROI for each of the individual tests. For eCommerce, we need to define not only conversion goals and success metrics, but also the micro-goals that led up to the sale.

For example, how many people clicked the "add to cart" button? Which individuals are playing a site video before they buy? What are your cart abandonment rates?

From all of this, you can create a hypothesis—an educated guess.

Every website out there is unique. That's why I recommend going through this process:

- Understand your qualitative data
- Understand your quantitative data
- Create a hypothesis
- Establish your personas with a unique value proposition
- Win quickly, scaling those wins to really improve your bottom line

This is the basic routine that we will go through for the five-step process in the Marketing Optimization System. It's all about that discovery process—creating a hypothesis, executing and creating tests, reviewing the analytics, and then scaling and growing over time.

You want to understand your customers and their problems. You want to create products to solve those problems, and you want to scale what works to improve your goals with short-term wins.

ACTION STEP 17:

List out the Five-Step process and describe how it relates to your online business.

Write out the micro-goals that will lead up to the sale.

What short-term wins can you accomplish in the next few weeks? List them.

STEP 1 – DISCOVERY

The secret to running successful split tests is doing a lot of research. We review quantitative and qualitative data to determine where we can find the biggest opportunities. Then we prioritize the changes we are going to make.

During this process, we establish what we can optimize immediately to get our quick wins using quantitative data. We do Google Analytics audits to review our top goals and our top landing pages, and we do revenue tracking, conversion tracking, and heatmap tracking.

We also utilize qualitative analysis. Understanding qualitative data helps us find some of the pains, problems, and desires of our ideal customers. This, in turn, enables us to find more opportunities to increase our overall eCommerce sales. The tools to do this used to be expensive and complicated to use. But now, great tools like UserTesting.com—where you can watch users/visitors travel through your site to understand exactly what's going on—are simple and readily available to anyone. UserTesting will help you understand how people are traveling through your websites, and you can break things down into a summary of what you've learned from the data. This will help you build out your wireframes based on insight and design feedback from those specific tests.

We'll also use heatmap software, Visual Website Optimizer, HotJar, or Inspectlet to see specifically where people are clicking and tools like Survey Monkey to review specific feedback customers and potential customers give us. As mentioned before, the survey can be added to many areas of your websites to automate the collection of qualitative feedback. Another tool that we'll use is Qualaroo to create a survey page that allows us to collect data from people who are leaving the website.

ACTION STEP 18:

Review the UserTesting.com videos you set up earlier.
List all the keywords, language, and observations
you gathered from watching the videos.

Review your SurveyMonkey feedback responses.
List what you learned from watching these videos.

Review your HotJar dashboard and review the
heatmaps and mouse tracking. List the observations
and problems that can be improved upon.

STEP 2 – HYPOTHESIS

Once we know where we need to start testing, we want to create a hypothesis. We'll use data and facts to come up with specific educated guesses. Then we'll outline an experiment to test the hypothesis and discuss how the results might impact the website.

Creating a hypothesis is very important because not only do you want to be able to track what is going on and measure properly, you also want to understand how it relates to each part of your business—how it affects your stakeholders, different business managers, and clients. After that, you need to figure out which of these different tasks takes priority.

Prioritizing can be done in different ways. I use a process created by Bryan Eisenberg. His approach encourages you to dig into the human element rather than looking at visitor feedback as qualitative data. In the planning mode, Bryan encourages you to answer these questions before running a test:

- Who are you trying to persuade?

- What action do you want them to take?

- What action do they want to take?

ConversionXL.com broke Bryan's process down into an easy to understand format:

Measure.

Design the test and define its parameters for success. Bryan recommends asking three more questions:

- What action do you want them to take, and where do we measure it?

- What pages do we want them to test?

- Where/how do we track success?

For example, you may have noticed in the past that many existing customers signed up because of the videos they have watched on your site. The goal of your pages may indeed be to get people to watch a specific video. So you set up a specific tracking to see if they're watching it or not. To get more people to watch it, you might try testing the video's actual thumbnail. You judge your success on whether or not you're converting from those who watch the video.

Improve.

Once you have the data, your next step is to improve on it. For example, if there are more people watching the video and converting, what does the video have that the page does not? If that "aha!" moment in the video is due to a testimonial or a success guarantee, is that specific information properly reflected on the page to encourage non-video watchers, too? Now that you have the data, learn from it and make improvements.

Prioritizing.

How many hours—development hours and man hours—will be necessary for this test to have an impact?

Impact.

This is the amount of time or the reduced cost that would change the event or produce a successful test. Are you increasing on the whole customer base or just a segment of it? Are you looking for a 1% or a 20% increase?

Resources.

What is the cost of the tools, people, and everything else associated with running the actual test? How much will the actual test cost?

The strategy of creating a hypothesis is taken from the scientific method. I have adapted Bryan Eisenberg's approach, combining it with a traditional hypotheses framework, to determine how to best organize each experiment idea.

Hypothesis Framework

A good hypothesis framework contains the following elements:

1. *Description of the observation to be explained*
   a. Who are you trying to persuade?
   b. What action do you want them to take?
   c. What action do they want to take?

2. *Description of the process hypothesized to cause the observation*
   a. What relevant observations are explained?
   b. What relevant observations are not explained?
   c. What observations are incompatible with the explanation?

3. *Description of how you will track success for the experiment*
   a. What goals and metrics are tracked during this experiment?
   b. If the hypothesis is validated, how would it affect the bottom line?
   c. What is the estimate for minimal success?

ACTION STEP 19:

Write a hypothesis for each of your top traffic landing pages. Describe the goals for each experiment.

Outline an experiment for each hypothesis and describe the efforts needed to accomplish the test.

Rank each experiment on a scale from 1-10, 10 being the most important. Determine which experiments are the most important in priority order.

STEP 3 – EXECUTION

First, you discovered your ideal target audience and defined who was visiting your website, and then you created a hypothesis for each experiment. Now you are going to develop the creative for the different variations in each experiment and set up the split testing using software like Visual Website Optimizer or Optimizely.

This is one of the most time-consuming sections of the process. Sometimes it can require a few different people to accomplish all the tasks needed. For example, when we're ready to create the mockups for the split testing variations, I develop wireframes for each variation. A wireframe is simply a black-and-white skeleton of a web page. The wireframes are turned into color designs using Photoshop. Once the color design is perfect, we can code the HTML needed to create the web pages. Then we can set up the split test directly in the testing software.

The experiments are added to the testing software and then set up to track a few main goals. The main goals that I usually set up for all tests include:

- Conversions – track visits to "Thank You" confirmation page

- Revenue – track revenue on each visit to "Thank You" confirmation page

- Clicks – track engagement with the page variation

After doing quality assurance testing of the experiments in all the necessary browsers, we will then begin the testing process for a specific segment of traffic. For example, if we're testing a product page from paid advertising, we will run tests for a desktop website differently than mobile-specific traffic.

Sometimes a test succeeds, and other times it fails. But it's important to analyze each success and failure in order to learn from them.

ACTION STEP 20:

In order of priority, create a black-and-white wireframe for each experiment.

Design, develop, and set up the first experiment in your split test software using Visual Website Optimizer or Optimizely.

Run an A/B split test experiment for a minimum
of 200 sales, 100 for each variation. If you are
running a test focused on lead generation, then
you want to reach a total of 500 leads collected,
or 250 leads for each variation.

STEP 4 – REVIEW
● ● ● ● ● ● ● ● ● ● ● ● ● ● ● ● ● ● ●

After the tests are successful, we need to be sure that it makes
sense to release the new creation on the live site as the new
baseline control. We will use a website data analyst to run
statistics to check that the new changes are going help our
conversion rates. Just because a split test wins doesn't always
mean you make more money.

Not only do we need to review the data from the finished test,
but we also need to determine if the winner will truly help the
bottom line growth of the business. There are many factors to
consider. How difficult will it be to implement into the
production website? What if the winner only corresponds to a
specific segment of traffic? We should test all segments to
ensure it produces the same results for all visitors on any
device they may be using.

ACTION STEP 21:

After your experiments have finished, use an analyst
to review your data and determine if the winning
results will help your business in the long run.

Have the analyst predict how these improvements
may affect your bottom line growth strategy.

> Set up metrics so that you can track
> this data easier in the future.

STEP 5 – SCALE

We're ready now to really grow our business and make more money. Once we determine what tests are helping to improve our conversion rates, increase sales, and generate more leads, we can then take what we learned and apply it to other areas of the eCommerce store. For example, if we learn that a new landing page headline helps increase conversion by 20 percent, we can then take that headline and create PPC ads with it. We can also test that high-converting headline on our homepage or category pages. This is how we scale all successful experiments.

ACTION STEP 22:

After determining which of your experiments should be made permanent on your live websites, it is now time to make them live across all your traffic.

Write a post-mortem for each experiment and determine how you can leverage these improvements for other areas of your websites.

Determine the main factors for why your experiments won or lost. For the winning experiments, list five ways you can scale these improvements to other marketing channels. Describe how they can be tested in your social media and your e-mail marketing campaigns.

PHASE 3 - BOTTOM LINE GROWTH PLAN

Just because a test wins for a specific segment of your website traffic doesn't mean it will win for every visitor coming to your website. That's why each test needs to be analyzed on a case-by-case basis. The average eCommerce website has five major templates:

1. Homepage

2. Category page

3. Product page

4. Contact page

5. Customer service pages like FAQ or return policy

There's also the shopping cart page and the checkout process. These are the major sections of the eCommerce site that determine the whole structure.

We test the highest traffic and most popular product pages on a small business eCommerce website. When we know that we have a new winning version, we can implement the successful elements into the default product templates. That way, all of the product pages now have the best converting elements across the entire website. This is how you take one winning page and scale it to grow your bottom line. The strategy can also work for your category templates, landing pages, campaign-specific microsites, and external websites.

ACTION STEP 23:

After you review the results of your experiments, determine how you can leverage this knowledge to improve other segments of your websites/visitor conversion.

Describe how you can use these improvements for your mobile and tablet experiences.

Describe how you can use these improvements to better change your paid ads and your organic search engine traffic.

PART TWO: CASE STUDIES: ECOMMERCE SMALL BUSINESS

Case Studies: eCommerce Small Business

I found plenty of areas for improvement on all of the case studies I'll be going through with you here. There are many effective parts, designs, and strategies, but I'll be telling you about the top ones. I'll identify specific priorities for each of the experiments based on what I learned from each test. With every testing, there will be losing experiments. But you tend to learn even more from your failures than your successes. I'll help you understand why tests may have lost. After you've read the case studies and have heard my tips and suggestions, you may come up with your own strategies that will work most effectively on your specific site.

CHAPTER - FOUR
CASE STUDY ONE - SELLING HEALTH AND FITNESS SUPPLEMENTS ONLINE

In 2004, I had the opportunity to work on a small business website that was using the eCommerce software, NetSuite. EnergyFirst.com is a health and fitness supplement company that sells whey protein powder, green drinks, and other vitamin supplements. It's run by a very successful entrepreneur, Gerry Morton. He was previously an Ironman and is very knowledgeable in the health and diet sector. He'd already had some major success, but the company needed to redesign their website. They came to me because I had a lot of experience in the health and fitness industry.

I really enjoyed working with Gerry. He was a successful entrepreneur, and he really inspired me. Gerry understood great design, but he was focused mostly on growth. This was a great opportunity for me to work on an up-and-coming eCommerce site and help them build out their brand while increasing their profit. It was one of the first websites I worked on where I was able to practice my HTML and CSS skills plus learn a lot more about conversion rate optimization.

Throughout my career, I'd worked with EnergyFirst.com a few times a year to help them with specific objectives. They would use me for small projects like custom landing pages and specific design changes. Eventually, I started to move into more of a consulting role where I helped them with specific strategies on how to make more money from their advertising campaigns.

They sell their products only online. You won't find their supplements in GNC, Wal-Mart, or any of those big companies. They focus on quality ingredients and great, all-natural products. They focused on proprietary health and fitness supplements, and their main products were whey protein powder, green drinks, and healthy energy drinks.

As the Internet has grown, we've helped the EnergyFirst.com site grow as well. I was excited when Gerry decided to rehire me in 2014 to help him increase his sales and leads for the upcoming holiday, Black Friday, and New Year's season.

PHASE 1 · STRATEGIC EVALUATION

It's very important to start with a clear strategic evaluation. You need to understand your company's objectives then determine what's working already and what needs the most attention. You don't want to make any assumptions about how to redesign your websites or tweak your marketing efforts. You should rely on data to direct each of the next steps.

After sitting down with Gerry, we were able to determine exactly what was going on with the website. We broke down specific goals for all the different types of pages then created a plan to iterate ways to success. That way there would be no guessing. We could simply test any hypothesis we had and get results. If a conversion test was a winner, then we could leverage that for the basis of a new hypothesis. But even if it was a loser, we could try to learn from what didn't work. This how you scale your business using compound growth tactics. Once we knew what was going on with the product and category pages, we were able to apply that to the homepage and get better results for all of the pages on the website. In the end, the homepage saw a decrease of 6.9% in bounce rate and the time on the page increased by 10%. This was a major achievement and dramatically increased the client's revenue.

The goals of this company were just like those of other eCommerce sites—increase total revenue, average order value, and the amount of leads and opt-ins that you get from e-mail lists. Goals also included improving new customer revenue, lifetime value, and leads for different types of devices—mobile versus tablet versus desktop—as well as decreasing the time to order, allowing new customers to purchase in a shorter amount of time.

We determined our objective was to optimize the top product pages to increase sales and reduce the CPA, which would return an overall increase in profit from Google AdWords campaigns. That way EnergyFirst.com could go into the holiday season with the best sales and lead generation process.

CASE STUDY ONE - PHASE 2 - MARKETING OPTIMIZATION SYSTEM

Creating a Marketing Optimization System is how you can create profitable online conversion testing plans, use web design to make more money, and optimize your lead generation to increase daily e-mail opt-ins. This case studies an online company that sells health supplements like whey protein, green drinks, and healthy energy drinks. We'd gathered a significant amount of data, so we now had a very clear and complete understanding of the customers, including how they were visiting our site and where they were going. We needed to create specific goals to increase conversion rate, improve revenue, and reduce their CPA, or cost per acquisition. We found through the testing that we were able to reach 100% confidence on the results that we got during a six-month period.

In the end, we were able to change all the advertising to point to the best performing pages and increase the bottom line. We found that the conversion rate on specific whey protein powder pages increased by 65%. It also increased the average order value by 48%. This result boosted the revenue per visitor by over $4 and resulted in an increase of over $2000 of revenue in twenty-one days. The CPA went down 50% as well. This helped EnergyFirst.com make more money while spending less on advertising.

In the MARKETING OPTIMIZATION SYSTEM, we use a five-step process to really understand what's going on with our site— where the people are going and what they're actually doing on each of the pages. It's based on the discovery, hypothesis, execution, review, and scaling process.

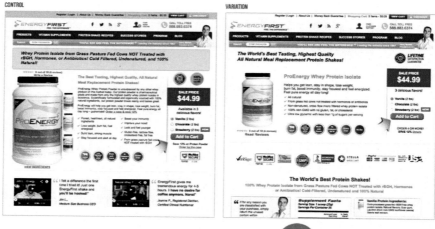

CASE STUDY ONE - STEP 1 - DISCOVERY

In the discovery process, we do both a quantitative and qualitative analysis. We put ourselves in the customer's shoes to figure out exactly what's going on so we can find areas of opportunity. In quantitative discovery, we learn specifically where people are going and then what they're doing on our websites.

The tools we used for quantitative were:

- Google Analytics

- eCommerce software called NetSuite

- Visual Website Optimizer – Split Testing & Revenue Tracking

Then for the qualitative aspect, we used:

- SurveyMonkey

- UserTesting

- Visual Website Optimizer - Heatmaps

Overall, the visitors to EnergyFirst.com were looking to do whatever they needed to stay healthy or to lose weight. We learned that the target audience was 42-58, was 55% female, and a large amount of the traffic used Safari. They had families and more than likely had a higher than average income. The voice of the customer was categorized as well—they didn't trust the online claims that most health websites made, they appreciated quality and service, and they wanted to be able to easily view the ingredients in each of the supplements. Next we used the qualitative discovery aspect using Visual Website Optimizer, User Testing, and Survey Monkey to get feedback from real customers.

With Visual Website Optimizer, we created heatmaps to figure out exactly where people were clicking.

We put ourselves in the customer's shoes to understand exactly how they were seeing our site, what browsers they were using, and where they were going. We got very specific feedback that helped us understand how to improve the site even further. This is essential to understanding the voice of the customer. The heatmap tool that I currently recommend is HotJar.

We set up specific survey tools using SurveyMonkey and added the links to different areas of our web pages, and we also used UserTesting. You want to bring the right people in to each of your tests based on the right personas. The trick to getting the best results is asking the right questions—specific questions related to first impressions, the checkout process, competitive analysis, returns, privacy, and trust. For EnergyFirst.com, we learned that people had a tendency to relate protein powder and supplements to the top drug store brands like GNC, Vitamin Shoppe, Drugstore.com, and even Amazon and Target. The site that stood out as a clean and efficient user experience was GNC, so we looked at GNC a lot—how they used coupons and how they organized their ingredients and benefits. We analyzed competitive product reviews to see why or why not people liked those products versus similar ones on EnergyFirst.com.

Here's a summary of what we learned from watching people use the website with UserTesting:

- Visitors wanted to know the product was the best tasting.

- Visitors wanted to know the product had the best quality ingredients and what they were.

- Visitors wanted to know the servings and how many calories were included in each of the whey protein shakes.

- They wanted to know what the health results would be for weight loss or everyday life. Did the product increase energy? Was it cost effective?

- They wanted to be convinced that there were no recurring fees.

- People also wanted to know more about the money back guarantee.

- Visitors wanted to know if the products were easy to return.

Eventually, you may run out of testing ideas, but you can always come back to your qualitative insight to find more experiment ideas. Take a look at each of the high traffic sections of your website and ask yourself if you've made your ideal customer's life better. Have you answered all of the questions that they've asked your customer service team? Are you giving them clear direction on what to do next? How can you make them not think and just take action? If you haven't clearly demonstrated answers to all those problems, then there is a still a lot of opportunity to test on each of the pages.

After gathering the data, we are now able to create a specific hypothesis and prioritize our next steps to increase each objective for our goals.

CASE STUDY ONE · STEP 2 – HYPOTHESIS

We gathered all of our data into our hypothesis and create specific educated guesses to determine what was going on for our conversion testing. After that, we prioritized a plan to make the biggest impact in the shortest amount of time.

Using the hypothesis framework, we organized each experiment:

1. *Description of the observation to be explained.*

   The whey protein powder is the top traffic landing page on EnergyFirst.com. It's also the bestselling product. 90% of the paid advertising traffic is sent to this page. Overall, we needed to improve the language and make the keywords stand out and be easier to understand. We wanted to display testimonials and customer reviews based on people's feedback. Customers also wanted to be able to compare the EnergyFirst.com brand to other products, so we needed to make that clearer.

   a. Who are you trying to persuade?

   Target audience was 55% female, ages 42-58, a large number using Safari. They had a family and more likely a higher income than average. They appreciated quality and service.

   b. What action do you want them to take?

   Visitors should add the item to the cart and complete the checkout process. If they are not ready to buy, they should want to download a free health guide.

c. What action do they want to take?

Customers simply want a healthy protein drink that helps them lose weight and increase their energy. They want to learn about the company but not be forced into buying something they don't need. They didn't trust the online claims that most health websites would make.

2. *Description of the process hypothesized to cause the observation.*

a. What relevant observations are explained?

Visitors like great taste, quality ingredients, and a comparison chart. Visitors like the shake recipes, but they are asking for specific calorie values.

The control page is very busy. There is a lot of information jammed into a small area. Overall, this caused a lot of confusion and didn't answer all of the user's questions and get them to convert. It had a lot of the right information—it just wasn't organized properly.

b. What relevant observations are not explained?

The text was hard to read, so we would be dividing the copy up into easy-to-read bullets. Make the top main panel area banner look less sales-focused, and tell people a story about why they should be using these particular products. Explain the difference between the results they'd get based on male versus female, gender-specific results. Show shake recipes that have certain calorie values. Reviews also became very important because they had been a hard to find. EnergyFirst.com has been around since 1997, but that language was hidden.

   c. What observations are incompatible with the explanation?

Customer reviews were apparent on the page but hard to understand. Some of the most important elements were on the page but hidden below the fold. People wanted to know gender-specific results.

Improve the average order value and decrease the time to order by making the vanilla protein the default product. Vanilla was the best-selling flavor.

Above the fold, a Better Business seal and a money back guarantee were missing.

3. *Describe how you will track success for the experiment.*

Reduce friction by giving visitors all the information they are looking for. Provide an easy-to-read format to drill down the information architecture.

   a. What goals and metrics are tracked during this experiment?

Three goals will be set up for each experiment.

     1. Conversion Rate = Visits to the thank you page divided by visitors
       a. This will also track total conversion per variation

     2. Revenue = Amount of revenue collected when reaching thank you page
       a. This will also track revenue per visitor
       b. This will also track revenue per conversion

     3. Engagement = Amount of people adding an item to the cart

       a. If the hypothesis is validated, how would it affect the bottom line?

If this experiment variation has an increased conversion and revenue per visitor, we can use the winning elements on other landing pages in the same format. By duplicating the winning elements across other top traffic landing pages, we can increase the overall conversion rate and average order value for all products.

b. What is the estimate for the success of this experiment?

The educated guess is that this experiment will increase the conversion for PPC AdWords campaigns by 15%.

Now we can create a list of prioritized tests based on elements in our hypothesis framework:

1. Whey Protein Powder Page – test headline, copy, and unique value proposition
2. Shopping Cart and Checkout – add security, guarantee, and instructions to purchase
3. Whey Protein Powder Page – reorganize the information so it's easy to read and addresses all the claims and frequently asked questions to make people feel more comfortable that this is the right product for them
4. Whey Protein Powder Page – add elements of social proof including testimonials, credibility logos, customer product reviews, and videos
5. Whey Protein Powder Page – redesign the page based on the winning elements in a modern design that uses larger fonts, bigger photos, and a comparison chart
6. Apply winning landing page to all other top product landing pages
7. Apply winning elements to the homepage, header navigation, and footer

CASE STUDY ONE · STEP 3 – EXECUTION

The execution phase is where we create all the tests by generating wireframes, design, and implementing the conversion testing.

Starting with the original Whey Protein Powder landing page, we began with a simple headline test. We use Visual Website Optimizer to set up each variation. In this case, it would be the control headline versus one test variation.

The control headline stated, "Whey Protein from Grass Pasture Fed Cows NOT Treated with rGBH, Hormones, or Antibiotics! Cold Filtered, Undenatured, and 100% Natural!" We set up a test, using our hypothesis to create a headline variation that said, "All Natural, Highest Quality Protein Shakes Great Taste – 5-Star Satisfaction." The test took about twenty-one days to run, and the new headline variation resulted in a 10% conversion lift. Not surprising since the control was pretty complex to start. Yet this told us we were moving in the right direction.

We determined that twenty-one days was the right amount of time to run the tests for EnergyFirst.com based on the amount of traffic that this website received during a three-week period. However, your website may only take two weeks to get a statistically confident result. If you have a lower traffic page, it may take even longer to see results from your A/B testing.

We began to come up with a lot of ideas to test. But we didn't want to change too much at one time. It made more sense to attack things at a slower pace so that we could create the Ideal M.A.P., building on each success element we found and making note of which tests might lose. The next step was to push the results even further. We took the exact same page information and created a new design with a clearer information hierarchy. This made the call to action areas obvious and organized the text so it was easier to read. The information architecture addressed the customers' concerns to make them feel more comfortable about ordering from EnergyFirst.com.

Some of the elements of the new design included:

1. A reassurance that they could check out with PayPal.

2. A relocation of the ingredients above the fold.

3. Increased visibility of the company guarantee and the supplement facts.

4. Addition of trust symbols—specific seals like the Better Business Bureau and McAfee.

The next test was designed to push the Whey Protein Powder page as far as we could before instituting a completely new design. We reorganized the information so it was easy to read, and we addressed all the claims and frequently asked questions to make people feel more comfortable that the product was the right one for them. We used Visual Website Optimizer to set up the new test for a twenty-one-day run. The three goals were all properly configured (Conversion, Revenue, and Engagement), and we were ready to begin the next step in the execution process. When we began the test, the results were flip-flopping all around, but we knew that was normal. After about five days, the results start to normalize, and one of the variations began to show clear results. After the first two weeks, we could clearly see that the new page was headed in the right direction. Then by day nineteen, we had achieved statistical significance, but we let the test run through the set time frame of twenty-one days.

It's important to let the test run for the set amount of time. If you take a test down in the middle, you will end up with misleading results. Even if a test is a failure, we need to ensure it runs long enough so we can review why it may have failed. This process can seem misleading at the beginning of a test, but you need to stay consistent on the length of time for all tests.

CASE STUDY ONE - STEP 4 – REVIEW

In the review phase, we were able to use an analyst/statistician to review our process and our results to ensure it would be beneficial for each client in the long run. We found that the conversion rate on specific whey protein powder pages increased by 65% and the average order value by 48%. This result increased the revenue per visitor by over $4 and resulted in a revenue increase of over $2000 in twenty-one days, an amazing result that we could replicate on other product pages.

Because we did a lot of qualitative and quantitative research, we knew that this was going to be a winner. It was clear to understand. The benefits were right there in front of you. There was support for our claims. We showed the calories and servings of the individual products, and we made the ingredients very clear and easy to compare to other protein products.

We also tested other headline versions, ultimately nailing down exactly what was happening on that particular page. Just testing the headline alone increased conversion by 10%, but once we combined everything together for the entire new page, it increased the conversion by 65% and upped the average order value by 48%.

The analyst said we had gathered enough data to determine the results of the specific tests for the whey protein powder landing pages. To our surprise, he came back after reviewing our data and told us that the test also resulted in the overall CPA going down by 50%, meaning we were spending less and generating a lot more profit. This particular product had 100% significance in beating out the old pages. This figure hadn't been included in our hypothesis, but Gerry was very happy to see more profit coming in and his conversion rates increasing.

This one test enabled us to determine exactly how to take this particular landing page and apply it to other inventory across their website.

After that, we were ready to move on to other areas of the website to start testing, including:

1. Shopping Cart and Checkout – add security, guarantee, and instructions to purchase

2. Completely new landing page design

3. Apply winning landing page to all other top product landing pages

4. Apply winning elements to the homepage, header navigation, and footer

CASE STUDY ONE - STEP 5 – SCALE

Once we know that a test is winning, we then move to the final phase where we scale and grow our ideas to other pages across the site.

We got a great result for our first few tests. The reason it went so well is because we'd put the time into doing great qualitative and quantitative research at the beginning. This is really where we got started. Quick wins can be easy if your site's not optimized. We wanted to break up the sections of the site and test different areas of opportunity next, and then do iterative experiments.

One of the biggest areas of opportunity was the navigation. The header navigation was broken up into different sections of the site for products, supplements, recipes, success stories, and program. This navigation model was working in general, but we learned that people wanted to get to the right products in fewer clicks.

So our new hypothesis was to create a "start here" page. A specific whey protein and other main products were put on the main navigation. We also added the Better Business Bureau and the McAfee Trust Seal to the header. Overall, this new navigation increased the total amount of clicks by 25.44%.

Now, from these two different tests, we thought we were on a great roll. We took what we had learned thus far and started to create completely new design layouts. Unfortunately, this particular test lost. It decreased conversion by 39.74%. Initially, we were unsure about why it hadn't worked, so we asked customers for feedback, and they said that it was too confusing a design overall.

This wasn't that bad, though. We tried again, creating completely different design layout based on what we had learned and where we'd failed. We were able to hone our new design based on customer feedback—creating a page that utilized a clear headline, provided social proof, and had easy-to-read text that led the eye right to a clear call-to-action area. This new test that we created increased the amount of conversion and the average order value by 56.37%—a dramatic increase. We were greatly surprised by the results.

Once we finished the landing page tests, we moved into homepage testing. We were able to define specific quick wins on some top traffic pages, and we created new pages based on those wins. Once we knew what was working, we had to scale those other products and landing pages so that their entire inventory got the same conversion rate improvements. We were also able to optimize the cart and checkout process to reduce cart abandonment rates. Lastly, we were able to take what we had learned and apply it to the homepage, thus reducing the bounce rate and increasing the amount of time spent on the website.

TEST: LANDING PAGE IMPROVEMENTS

56% CONVERSION IMPROVEMENT

CASE STUDY ONE -
PHASE 3 – BOTTOM LINE GROWTH PLAN

Once you know what's winning on one page, leverage that for other top traffic to increase your bottom line.

The results of this testing process really started to pay off. We learned that our efforts increased the average order value by 30% and the conversion rate by 56.4%. The revenue per visitor increased as well. Once we knew exactly what was going on with one page, we were able to leverage that and scale and grow. That's how we figured out how to increase the lifetime value of their customers. One of the things we found was that more people wanted to buy more than one bottle of whey protein powder at a time. We went through every area of "add to cart" to ensure that there was the ability to add more than one item to the cart. We also checked that all product pages had a quantity field next to each item. Adding the quantity field increased the average order value because customers could save on larger orders.

Once we knew what was happening on the one page, we were then able to scale it out to all of the other landing pages. We applied it to their green drink landing page, to their energy drink landing page, and then to their Omega oil product landing page. We also determined ways to figure out how to leverage their existing advertising into their Facebook and Google Ad Words. We tested ads with specific headlines that worked well. We also tested imagery from the specific landing pages. We now had an arsenal!

We used those ads targeted on competitive ads and also used headlines from our UserTesting and our feedback to learn how we could improve our Google AdWords even further. In the end, we saw an increase in the bottom line of EnergyFirst.com. In the past, we would have had only five out of ten winning tests, but because we had gone through a great amount of research doing qualitative and quantitative analysis, we were able to achieve a bigger impact and have more consistent winning tests through our conversion testing.

Using the Marketing Optimization System, we were able to increase the amount of orders from the Whey Protein Page from an average of 130 sales per month to over 280 sales per month. This resulted in the overall CPA going down by 50%, meaning we were spending less and generating a lot more profit. Additionally, the improvements we made to the lead generation strategy tripled the amount of new e-mail opt-ins we collected daily.

To learn more about the results of this entire project, visit the website: SBBMO.com

TEST: HOMEPAGE REDESIGN

CONTROL

VARIATION

BOUNCE RATE DECREASE

CHAPTER - FIVE

CASE STUDY TWO - MAKING E-LEARNING COURSES PROFITABLE

This next case study will show you how we took the winning strategy from one websites and scaled it to another websites to grow the bottom line for the entire business fleet of websites.

Aside from traditional eCommerce websites, I also work with many companies that use eCommerce platforms to sell their online software services. MyTaxCoursesOnline.com is a websites that was started by a successful entrepreneur, Derek Woryn. All of the courses they create are sold using the eCommerce software Magento.

This project showed that online learning is quickly replacing the traditional classroom environment for professional continuing education and certifications. As an accomplished expert in e-Learning Course Development, Derek Woryn had a vision to convert traditional trainings into online courses that can be done anytime, anywhere, and at your convenience, giving professionals the time they need to focus on achieving overall business goals.

Here I will show you how we took the winning elements of one site and applied them to several of their other websites and landing pages, resulting in increased revenue and leads while decreasing cart abandonment rates.

CASE STUDY TWO -
PHASE 1 - STRATEGIC EVALUATION

Derek and I got on a call and he said, "We have several courses for people in the tax industry, and these courses are designed to either help them get a certain certification to do taxes or provide them the continuing education necessary for them to renew their license every year. My opinion of our homepage is that it kind of sucks, but I'm only saying that from a design standpoint. From a conversion standpoint, it may be good just because it's simple."

Originally the company was interested in creating a couple of landing pages for an online tax course program and split testing those—an A and a B design—to see which ones converted better. They were also interested in split testing the homepage designs to try and refine the process.

We needed to analyze the traffic patterns and determine where some of the problems were in the whole process. Usually in that three-week process, once we determined the traffic patterns and where people were falling off and where the problems were, we could come up with the top five quick wins for conversion improvements.

I also thought that the site needed to be grounded in the future by either a spokesperson or a well-known figure or even just a picture—but it certainly needed some type of social proof. The site was missing all of those aspects that are huge influencers in getting someone to purchase something for $149.

CASE STUDY TWO - PHASE 2 - MARKETING OPTIMIZATION SYSTEM

The site we began to improve was MyTaxCoursesOnline.com.

We determined that the quick win to improve the site would be to add a money-back guarantee seal to the homepage and then apply that seal to the product pages as well. The site also had a very vague unique value proposition, so we wanted to work on their headlines to ensure that people understood exactly what products and services they offered. The next move was to take their product page and test it as a landing page. Lastly, we wanted to determine how many people were going through the mobile and tablet experience and ensure it was easy for them to sign up via those venues.

CASE STUDY TWO - STEP 1 – DISCOVERY

After a qualitative and quantitative analysis, we determined the area with the largest opportunity to increase their sales and leads and came up with a number of improvements to create some interesting hypotheses.

The tools we used for quantitative was:

- Google Analytics
- Visual Website Optimizer
- eCommerce software called Magento

Then for the qualitative aspect, we used:

- SurveyMonkey
- UserTesting

- Inspectlet
- CrazyEgg

They were bringing all their leads through Infusionsoft, and they had a great model that we could easily improve upon. Their biggest opportunity was finding the areas of improvement and making the most of their existing traffic to leverage those visitors and increase the amount of revenue they made. We found that just by going through the actual user experience as if we were a customer, there were a lot of improvements that could be made.

We used UserTesting.com to determine exactly where people were having problems with the site and what information was missing. We also found the biggest opportunity to be in the mobile aspect. The amount of mobile traffic was only about 25% at the start, but every month we started to see continuous improvement in the mobile experience. We also needed to come up with a Mobile Marketing Optimization System for their marketing efforts. If you're interested in a mobile CRO book, please email alex@alexdesigns.com.

Because we knew exactly what Internet browsers and versions people were using, we learned a lot about how to make major changes for MyTaxCoursesOnline.com We also determined the referral traffic and what people were truly interested in.

We took a look at their top traffic landing pages and determined that the majority of traffic and revenue came from the homepage, but the other two or three high traffic pages included the individual product page. There was also a lot of drop-off within the checkout process.

From our research in UserTesting, we knew exactly what was going on. People gave feedback that MyTaxCourseOnline.com looked like an amateur site. It was dated. People were confused about the different courses, and they wanted to see more testimonials. This helped us build our hypothesis to make changes to the existing pages.

We investigated further by using different tools like Inspectlet and heatmap tracking from Visual Website Optimizer. We determined exactly where people were going and what they were clicking on. We saw how people were flowing through the page. The majority of people were going to the exam pages, but once they got there, they were confused about how to check out.

CASE STUDY TWO - STEP 2 – HYPOTHESES

Now we had enough data to create our hypotheses for testing. The goal was to stop making people think, removing friction as much as possible. We wanted to ensure that people understood what they were purchasing. We'd used Visual Website Optimizer to watch people visit the top landing pages and click on certain elements on the heatmaps, so we knew what pages they were visiting and what they were actually clicking on.

We then used the hypothesis framework to organize each experiment:

1. *Description of the observation to be explained.*

   The homepage is the top traffic landing page on MyTaxCoursesOnline.com. 70% of the direct traffic is sent from e-mail marketing campaigns. The main issue was that the homepage design looked very amateur. The shopping cart and checkout process needed to be improved to decrease their cart abandonment rates.

   a. Who are you trying to persuade?

      Target customers were mostly men, aged 38 to 55 (around 90% of the total demographic). Visitors were looking to achieve their educational and career goals by looking for continuing competency programs. They were eager to take the courses quickly. They had a higher than average income.

b. What action do you want them to take?

Visitors should add the item to the cart and complete the checkout process. If they were not ready to buy, they should want to opt-in to a free course.

c. What action do they want to take?

Visitors wanted to take a course and be guaranteed that they would pass the test. Otherwise, they wanted their money back.

2. *Description of the process hypothesized to cause the observation.*

a. What relevant observations are explained?

The websites courses had a great money back guarantee, but it was hidden and didn't ensure the customer that they were guaranteed to pass the course. The websites was mobile friendly, but the layout was smushing all the content together.

There were too many options on the homepage. People were confused about all the different choices.

There were many great accreditations that the company had, but they were not clearly displayed above the fold for the user. Also, the Better Business Bureau logo was hidden in the footer area.

b. What relevant observations are not explained?

The homepages did not have a clear and unique value proposition. Visitors were confused about what to do next and why they should use the websites to take these courses.

There was a lack of social proof, and the site wasn't showing how others had gotten results with the same course. We needed to add testimonials and increase the credibility of their offerings. There was also a lack of clear FAQs on the homepage and product detail pages.

There was no goal tracking set up in Google Analytics.

c. What observations are incompatible with the explanation?

The mobile experience was messy and unorganized. With mobile traffic increasing monthly, the screens needed a lot of work to organize the information in an easy-to-understand way.

3. *Describe how you will track success for the experiment.*

The overall goal for the eCommerce site was to optimize for increased conversion, increased average order value, and increased lifetime value. We also wanted to increase the amount of leads that we generated and decrease the time to purchase.

a. What goals and metrics are tracked during this experiment?

Three goals will be set up for each experiment.

1. Conversion Rate = Visits to the thank you page divided by visitors
   a. This will also track total conversion per variation

2. Revenue = Amount of revenue collected when reaching thank you page
   a. This will also track revenue per visitor
   b. This will also track revenue per conversion

3. Engagement = Amount of people adding an item to the cart

a. If the hypothesis is validated, how would it affect the bottom line?

If this experimental variation has an increased conversion and revenue per visitor, we can use the winning elements in the same format on other landing pages. By duplicating the winning elements across other top traffic landing pages, we can increase the overall conversion rate and average order value for all products.

b. What is the estimate for the success of this experiment?

The educated guess is that this experiment will increase the conversion for natural search traffic by 10%.

Now we can create a list of prioritized tests based on elements in our hypothesis framework:

1. MyTaxCoursesOnline.com Homepage Improvements – Decrease time to order by displaying guarantee. Increase credibility by putting Better Business Bureau and other accreditations in the header area.

2. MyTaxCoursesOnline.com Product Pages – Add special offer next to the call to action buttons to increase "add to cart" clicks. Make phone number clickable in mobile and add the guarantee, accreditation, and frequently asked questions above the fold.

3. MyTaxCoursesOnline.com Mobile Experience – Increase leads and sales phone calls.

4. MyTaxCoursesOnline.com Shopping Cart & Checkout Improvements

5. MichiganBuildersLicence.com
   Homepage Improvements – Decrease time to order

6. MichiganBuildersLicence.com
   Shopping Cart & Checkout Improvements

CASE STUDY TWO · STEP 3 – EXECUTION

We knew we needed to begin by improving the MyTaxCoursesOnline.com homepage. The idea was to start with a few small tests to get a better idea of the bigger picture and then move to the individual product pages and leverage what we had learned from the homepage research and split testing.

Their original homepage was very vague and confusing. It was hard to understand what you were looking for. The page was also unappealing and outdated. We created an initial wireframe, reorganized the page, placed clear action steps above the fold, posted a clear value proposition, and added a clear headline and easy-to-read bullets. We also ensured that the guarantee was clear and easy to understand. Customers had a thirty-day money back guarantee—if they didn't pass the tax training, they got their money back. We leveraged the existing testimonials and success stories to establish trust.

Next we began making improvements to the MyTaxCoursesOnline.com product pages. These pages had very similar problems to the homepage. Our goal was to update the product pages along with the guarantee, reinforcing value propositions with video and other elements to convince people to convert.

There was a lot of opportunity to improve the checkout process and decrease cart abandonment rates. The company was not doing a very good job of understanding where people were dropping off. That's the reason you must put yourself in your customers' shoes—so you can see what it's like to try to check out and buy the products. As we continued to improve the shopping cart experience, we let customers know they were in a secure shopping experience by adding a lock symbol next to the shopping cart title.

People were having a lot of problems in the mobile and tablet experiences. We needed to implement a Mobile Marketing Optimization System to help the company improve their revenue, sales, and growth in this area. If visitors weren't interested in signing up during their mobile experience, we needed to get them to fill out a lead generation form and send them in the direction of the company's Infusionsoft email marketing campaign.

There were a lot of confusing navigational items in their header. The same with the footer—it lacked information. We mocked up improvements to the header and footer areas.

There were many great accreditations that the company had, but they were not clearly displayed above the fold for the user. The Better Business Bureau logo was hidden in the footer area.

There was a lack of social proof, and the site was not displaying the results of others from the course. We needed to add testimonials and increase the credibility of their offerings. There was also a lack of clear FAQs on the homepage and product detail pages.

CASE STUDY TWO - STEP 4 – REVIEW

We designed a new homepage and created many different pages for the company and then set it up for testing using Visual Website Optimizer. Adding the guarantee, the testimonials, and the reformatted homepage with the new value proposition, headlines, and easy-to-read bullets increased the conversion of the new homepage by 73%.

After posting of the redesigned homepage, we immediately saw an increase in sales. We doubled the company's frequency in sales to reach more than a 3% conversion rate. The next step of testing was to take what we'd learned on the homepage and apply it to the product-specific pages.

We learned that many people were going to other web pages and were really confused about how to get back to the courses. There were a lot of navigational issues. We were able to fix that easily by improving the overall user experience.

We made some additional changes to the shopping cart and checkout pages. The fields had been very hard to see. There weren't any seals for security. The "place order" button was very confusing because it was the same color as all the other buttons. We made a lot of changes to the cart and checkout process, resulting in a 50% reduction in the cart abandonment rate.

Using the Marketing Optimization System, we were able to increase MyTaxCoursesOnline.com daily sales from fifteen to over fifty sales per day.

TEST: HOMEPAGE REDESIGN

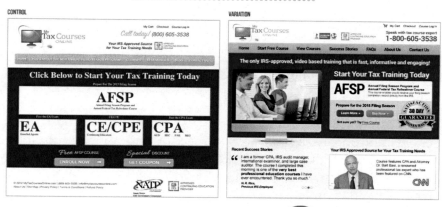

73% CONVERSION INCREASE

CASE STUDY TWO - STEP 5 – SCALE

We recognized that MyTaxCoursesOnline.com had the same problems from one website to another, so we were able to easily jump into a hypothesis and start executing specific tests. Once we knew what was going on with one websites, we were able to apply the same lessons to the others within the CBT family. With MichiganBuildersLicense.com, we immediately noticed that they were missing the guarantee, the value proposition was a little bit vague, and the user experience was very confusing. Also the web design, as with the other one, was very amateur and looked quite dated.

We took what we had already learned and applied it to the product specific pages—adding the guarantee, the testimonials, and improved video. That helped increase the conversion even further, another 25%.

CASE STUDY TWO –
PHASE 3 · BOTTOM LINE GROWTH PLAN

The changes we made have helped the company dramatically improve their bottom line.

In summary, we were able to see some amazing results, especially on MyTaxCoursesOnline.com and MichiganBuilders License.com. Using the Marketing Optimization System, we were able to increase MyTaxCoursesOnline.com daily sales from 15 new daily customers to over 50 sales per day. On MichiganBuildersLicense.com websites, sales increased from 150 new customers to 450 sales per month.

To learn more about the results of this entire project, visit the website: SBBMO.com

TEST: HOMEPAGE REDESIGN

CONTROL

VARIATION

300+ NEW CUSTOMERS PER MONTH

CHAPTER - SIX

CASE STUDY THREE - TAKING FOOD DELIVERY ORDERS ONLINE

In 2014, I was in between projects and getting ramped up for the upcoming holiday eCommerce season when I received a new lead from Simon Gorman in my e-mail inbox. It was a simple request from the contact form on my website that read, "Interested in a comprehensive CRO project for our online store, www.wisechoicemarket.com." Wise Choice Market is an eCommerce site that sells organic and health-conscious, non-GMO food. They'd recently done a site redesign and were not getting the results they'd expected.

Simon gave me his thoughts for his website. "My instinct tells me that we get a lot of abandonments because of the shipping cost. Our frozen foods can be expensive to ship because we use dry ice. We need to show profit while trying to keep shipping costs down. That's number one, and the second thing is, again, before you get to the stage of actually building the testing, bear in mind that we use Bigcommerce as our platform."

I explained to Simon that Bigcommerce is like any other platform—whether it's Magento, Shopify, or another hosted eCommerce solution—in that it has its restrictions and its limits. We needed to be careful that whatever we created could actually be implemented on that platform afterward. I told him that Marketing Optimization Systems starts with a discovery process where we track baseline sales and leads. Then we collect data using heatmaps, UserTesting, and surveys. I'd gather all the findings together in a comprehensive plan for him and complete a video walkthrough that would explain everything in detail. In the video, I'd recommend the top quick wins for his website and a list of long-term improvements we could work on together. Then we'd meet weekly to set our objectives.

Simon agreed to my proposal, and we embarked on a new business relationship, with me guiding them to make more money, generate more leads, and maximize their ROI.

CASE STUDY THREE · PHASE 1 – STRATEGIC EVALUATION

Wise Choice Market had done a little bit of testing themselves in the past using Optimizely. You could say it was prematurely optimized as they had only scratched the surface. They had also gotten Google Analytics working properly to track their goals and eCommerce conversions and were about to implement a customer reviews software called Yotpo.

But Simon had other concerns. He asked me, "Is our website generating enough traffic to complete conversion testing? We're looking at traffic around between fifteen and twenty thousand unique visitors a month. Is that enough for you to work with? We had decided to get the conversion rate as high as possible before spending a lot of money on Google AdWords." I told Simon that, yes, they had enough traffic to get started with the optimization process, and that he had been wise to increase conversion rates before wasting too much money.

Simon was especially interested in finding out the number of people who navigated through their website. As soon as we knew what people were already doing, we could then find out exactly where they were clicking, what pages that they were going to, specific items they were clicking on—and then we could interrupt those patterns. The tool I use for mouse tracking and heatmaps is called HotJar. This is where we'd find the quick wins to perform iterative experiments, hoping to result in immediate improvements.

There was a lot of information on Simon's website *before* the products actually started. That could be good in a way, but it did take a bit of effort to get to some of the products, so I was curious to watch others go through the site to find a specific item. There were certainly some navigation issues in both the header and left navigation. In addition, there was also the issue of telling people exactly what to buy and answering their top frequently asked questions without them getting lost. There was certainly a lot of opportunity for improvement.

Next, I asked Simon, "What are your best-selling items? What do people buy first, and what do people buy most?"

Simon answered, "That, by far, would be our bone broth. That's why we put it at the top. The bone broth category page has the biggest traffic—twice as much traffic as the homepage. So in terms of page views per month, I think it's the broth category page, then the homepage, and then the fermented vegetables category."

Simon wanted to ensure that the end result of our efforts would mean a higher conversion rate—always our ultimate goal. Obviously we want to increase the sales, the conversion rates, and the leads.

Then I asked Simon if there were any other expectations he wanted me to meet.

He said, "I guess the basic one would be that I'd like the results to be backed up by data so that I actually know that if we change A to A + B, it's because of whatever that micro-goal might be. That's number one. I don't really want to rely on general best practices because they may not be right for us. We've got a very specific audience, and we cater to a very specific market. They're quite strict in what they expect in their foods. What's best practice for Amazon or eBay is not necessarily best practice for our audience, so whatever changes we make, they must be supported by data."

We can guess at what we should test first, but until we drill through the data to figure out where the biggest opportunity is, it will always be *just* a guess. Usually, when it comes down to food, the one or two things people question when arriving at a particular product page are related to credibility and trust.

CASE STUDY THREE –
PHASE 2 - MARKETING OPTIMIZATION SYSTEM

The main goal of an eCommerce website is to generate revenue, but what are the micro-goals? What are those other key performance indicators that are most important to improve the growth of the eCommerce site?

This client initially came to me concerned about spending money on the website because it had been ineffective in the past. They'd been online a while and knew that their conversion rate should be a lot higher. We needed to create a system to dramatically increase their conversions before the owner started spending money on new marketing campaigns. They had a limited budget and limited time, so if they didn't see an immediate impact or immediate return on investment, then they'd probably be wasting a lot of money.

We wanted to understand what the company's upfront revenue was, what the average lifetime value of each customer was, and how to increase that lifetime value overall. We also wanted to figure out ways to shorten the ordering time because, at the time, there were lots of new visitors coming to this site due to new health trends.

CASE STUDY THREE - STEP 1 – DISCOVERY

Again, in the discovery process, we want to put ourselves in the customer's shoes and understand exactly what's going on in the qualitative and qualitative realms. We want to define the specific tools that we're going to use.

The tools we used for quantitative were:

- Google Analytics
- Visual Website Optimizer
- LeadPages
- eCommerce software called Bigcommerce

Then for the qualitative aspect, we used:

- SurveyMonkey
- UserTesting
- HotJar

We learned it was important to customers that a non-GMO seal was prominently displayed, that they wanted quality food that they could make at home, and that they were busy and really just wanted convenience and were willing to pay for it. That's where we started to dig into our qualitative aspect.

Using qualitative insight tools, we were able to analyze feedback from the customers or create specific surveys asking them for feedback about what products they may want to see on the site. We also asked them open-ended questions to gather data for our conversion testing. This would help us point out specific patterns and keywords that we could use in our marketing material.

In UserTesting, we want to be sure to screen the customers so that we brought the right people into the right tests. In this case, we screened the audience and brought in only users who bought organic groceries online. The next question we asked them was if they knew what bone broth was. That way, we could watch only the people going through our site who were interested in bone broth. We wanted to gather their first impressions and watch them go through our checkout process, through our competitors, through different Google search queries. We wanted find out if they believed in us. Did they trust us? Did they believe they were able to return their products? The last question we asked was if they had a magic wand, how would they improve the overall Wise Choice Market experience?

Let your customers tell you what is wrong with your site. Through this, we learned the specific keywords that became very important to us—delicious stew, gourmet, nutritious, farmer's market, delivered, convenience, quality ingredients. We also found out what customers *didn't* like. Apparently, the buttons were confusing in the add-to-cart area, and the e-mail fields looked too much like an ad.

In UserTesting, we were able to send people through different devices and watch them go through different experiences. We found that the mobile experience of Wise Choice Market had much room for improvement. Overall, it was confusing. It was also hard to check out and complete a final purchase. Even though some people may do research on a mobile and then later do the actual buying on a tablet, we still want to ensure that mobile is a simple experience. We wanted people's questions to be answered on all of the different landing pages and wanted to reduce the cart abandonment rates during the checkout process. Lastly, there were no clear reviews or any social engagement anywhere on the site, and we needed to fix that.

Probably the biggest area of opportunity for non-optimized sites is knowing the top traffic landing pages. We learned that the bone broth category page was receiving a lot more traffic than any other page out there, and it was clear that all we had to do was tweak that page just a little bit to see some dramatic results. All we had to do was shift some elements around to achieve an immediate increase in conversion.

CASE STUDY THREE - STEP 2 – HYPOTHESES

After the discovery step, we had enough data to create our specific hypotheses that we could begin to test. Our goal was to stop making people think, to remove as much friction as possible. We wanted to remove all of the gimmicky aspects and make sure that people understood what they were purchasing.

We then used the hypothesis framework to organize each experiment:

1. *Description of the observation to be explained.*

   The bone broth category page was the top traffic landing page on WiseChoiceMarket.com. It was also the bestselling product. 70% of the direct traffic was sent to this page. The main issue was that the product images and related calls to action were below the screen fold and out of sight of each of the visitors. By moving the products above the fold, we would ensure that more bone broth purchases would take place immediately.

   a. Who are you trying to persuade?

   Target customers were mostly women, aged 42 to 58 (around 80% of the total demographic) who had families and were concerned about the quality of food they were giving to their family. We found that the majority of people who visited the site were cooking enthusiasts who enjoyed quality ingredients and were part of a family with a higher income. More than half of them were using Internet Explorer. They were a very health-conscious population.

b. What action do you want them to take?

Visitors should add the item to the cart and complete the checkout process. If they aren't ready to buy, they should want to download a free recipe guide.

c. What action do they want to take?

Visitors wanted to learn about the health benefits of bone broth. If they were ready and could afford the product, they would buy it.

2. *Description of the process hypothesized to cause the observation.*

a. What relevant observations are explained?

Bone broth was listed on the page with a clear description of the product.

b. What relevant observations are not explained?

They wanted samplers so that they could sample the product before making bigger purchases. Their first impression was that the technology seemed a little unreliable, and they couldn't find where they could sign up for the newsletter. They were impressed with how the delivery process worked for the perishable organic ingredients. They understood how dry ice worked and that it was necessary for the delivered food to be super fresh. We also found out that people didn't believe the claims the company was making about organic or non-GMO foods—both things that are very important to this particular persona.

c. What observations are incompatible with the explanation?

The bone broth category section did not clearly show how and why to purchase the products. We discovered that all we had to do was move some elements around to realize an immediate increase in conversion.

3. *Describe how you will track success for the experiment.*

The overall goal for the eCommerce site was to optimize for increased conversion, increased average order value, and increased lifetime value. We also wanted to increase the amount of leads generated and decrease the time for customers to purchase.

a. What goals and metrics are tracked during this experiment?

Three goals will be set up for each experiment.

1. Conversion Rate = Visits to the thank you page divided by visitors

   a. This will also track total conversion per variation

2. Revenue = Amount of revenue collected when reaching thank you page

   a. This will also track revenue per visitor

   b. This will also track revenue per conversion

3. Engagement = Amount of people adding an item to the cart

   a. If the hypothesis is validated, how would it affect the bottom line?

If this experiment shows an increased conversion and revenue per visitor, we can put the winning elements to use on other landing pages in the same format. By duplicating the winning elements across other top traffic landing pages, we can increase the overall conversion rate and average order value for all products.

c. What is the estimate for the success of this experiment?

The educated guess is that this experiment will increase the conversion for natural search traffic by 10%.

Now we can create a list of prioritized tests based on elements in our hypothesis framework:

1. Bone Broth Category – Move product calls to action above the fold

2. Seals for Organic, Non-GMO, and so on – Create images of seals for health concerns

3. Shopping Cart Abandonment Improvements –Security seals, credibility, and instructions

4. Add Recipe Guide Download Links - Increase leads from non-converting traffic

5. Custom PPC Landing Pages – Create microsite for bone broth AdWords traffic

6. Homepage Improvements – Add clear UVP, product images, and social proof

We devised a great plan based on the prioritization of our top tests, different landing pages, areas of opportunity, revenue amount, and web traffic pages. We had determined that the bone broth page had the biggest area of opportunity, and our hypothesis was that people were confused about how to add an item to the cart and that the company's main product was appearing below the fold.

CASE STUDY THREE - STEP 3 – EXECUTION

Our next step was to wireframe each hypothesis, create the needed designs, code any HTML, and set up the conversion testing to validate the experiments.

After having an analyst review the entire process, we learned that everything we had done so far was on the right track. Again, it was all because of the qualitative and quantitative research we'd done to figure out the proper message to give to the proper person in the proper experience on the proper device. Segmentation has become more important than ever. If people are viewing your site in a mobile experience, be sure to give them the correct experience. If people are on a tablet, give them the right information. In the long run, people will be happier with your brand.

The bone broth category was the first experiment that we would run. Our goal was simply to move product calls to action above the fold. Our educated guess was that our conversion would increase by 10%. All we had to do was take the elements from below the fold and move them to the top. This was a very simple test that didn't take long to set up using Visual Website Optimizer. Our test resulted in a 30.62% increase in conversion, just from moving an element to the top of the page and shifting the products above the fold. Once we knew that was a winner, we knew we were on track to continue with further conversion testing.

TEST: MOVE CTA BUTTONS ABOVE FOLD

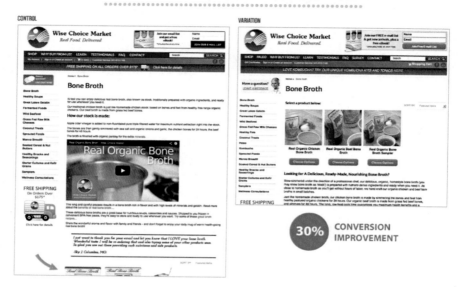

Our next hypothesis was that people did not believe that the company sold non-GMO, organic, or quality ingredients. To test this hypothesis, we created specific seals for organic, non-GMO, paleo, and nutrient-dense qualities. The goal was for the visitor to clearly understand that these were the highest quality food items and that they could trust Wise Choice Market. We added the seals to the corresponding category pages and set up our test using Visual Website Optimizer for the three goals we wanted to measure. The test resulted in a 4.5% increase in average order value.

These small changes *do* make a difference, especially in the long term. We took the seals we used on those category pages and started applying them to the individual product pages. Simply adding those seals increased the product page conversions by 12.4%. This is where we start to see that bottom line growth—when we take a winning element from one area and apply it to many different areas of a website. In this manner, we ensure that each template on your eCommerce site has the best conversion elements possible.

Before we moved on to additional testing, we sat down with an analyst to determine exactly how to proceed and whether the changes were worth implementing permanently.

TEST: ADD SEALS TO PRODUCT PAGE

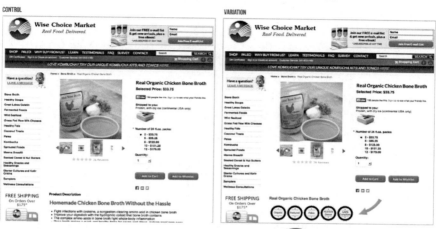

12% CONVERSION IMPROVEMENT

CASE STUDY THREE - STEP 4 – REVIEW

When a test is finished, we want to review it carefully to ensure that it's truly a winner before we move on to the next phase, scaling and growing your bottom line. Once we know that something is winning and worth implementing, we can then spread those results to other pages to dramatically grow our bottom line.

In the Wise Choice Market example, we determined there was still a lot of improvement that could be made to the bone broth category pages. This helped determine a new project to create custom PPC Landing Pages for the bone broth website. We found that many people were coming to the bone broth pages, but they were confused by the options for other products. So this gave me the idea to create a microsite for bone broth AdWords Traffic.

The next test we wanted to do was on segmenting out paid advertising. Paid advertising was one of the biggest areas of opportunity because the client was concerned about spending money without seeing a good return on investment. Initially, we set up a new pay-per-click landing page based on all the different things we'd learned. Unfortunately, the first test we ran had a decrease of 39% in conversion, but we didn't just drop the ball there. We learned from what we'd done, and we continued to move forward, realizing that this project needed more work before we could retest it again.

TEST: LANDING PAGE REDESIGN

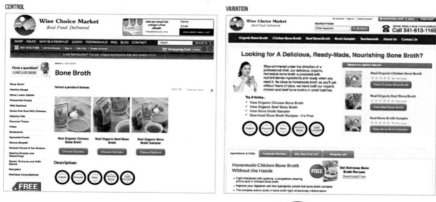

39% CONVERSION DECREASE

Many visitors would return to the website multiple times before finally making a purchase. This showed that we needed to start a retargeting marketing campaign especially for people who abandoned the shopping cart and checkout process.

It was also obvious that we needed a better plan to collect for e-mail opt-in, so we moved to make lead generation a top priority for the next few projects. Especially on the mobile experience, we learned that many visitors were researching products on their mobile phone but not completing a final order. Our main goal for mobile would now shift to collecting e-mail opt-in leads.

CASE STUDY THREE · STEP 5 – SCALE

As we continued to roll on, we started to see that all we had to do now was continue that system. We had to take what was working from all of those previous tests and apply them to different areas of the site. We'd already been working on the category pages for a few weeks. Now it was time to take those wins and apply them to the product pages.

The next test we were ready to run was all about ingredients and videos. People consume content in many different ways. Some people watch videos, and some people read, but you want to have it *all* available so you can appeal to every buyer modality. In the case of Wise Choice Marketing, the original website concept had all the information there—it was just hard to see and was very confusing. The visual hierarchy wasn't there, so our hypothesis was to test this new information architecture with a nutrition facts area that was clean and easy to read.

This test was one of our biggest winners. Just taking that information and reorganizing it in the right way increased the total conversion by 21.25%. It also increased the average order value of those individual product pages by 70.85%, a major win for us going forward because we knew we were on track for something really big. We knew there was so much more opportunity, especially in the areas of navigational elements, cart checkout process, and the homepage.

We had a great plan in place. We had five winning tests before getting our first loser. That's an excellent run rate. We knew we still had a lot more opportunity for growth—we hadn't even touched the lead generation process or the homepage. Those were still untapped areas for future improvement.

CASE STUDY THREE · PHASE 3 – BOTTOM LINE GROWTH PLAN

The marketing optimization system is all about getting a bigger impact by cutting through the clutter of all the different tools and systems. Marketing tools have made us more efficient, but they don't understand human behavior. That's our job. We must also create specific baselines for our revenue and conversion. Then we can scale our wins even further to grow the bottom line for a total conversion lift.

Another major focus area for WiseChoiceMarket.com was increasing the amount of leads and e-mail opt-ins they collected on a daily basis. The company was reluctant to run Facebook and lead generation promotions because they just weren't generating enough new leads. We scoped out the ideal click M.A.P. to determine how to maximize lead generation and e-mail opt-ins. The funnel we decided to create was based on their bestselling product, bone broth. We determined that offering a bone broth recipe guide as a free giveaway for the e-mail opt-in landing pages would be the best scenario to begin with. We used LeadPages, a simple-to-use landing page creation tool, to create a few different landing pages from which we could test our Facebook marketing programs. Then we applied some knowledge we'd gained from a previous test. The new landing page for lead generation resulted in a conversion of 75% for targeted Facebook campaigns. This new process would increase the daily e-mail collected from just a few entries to over 100 new e-mails per day.

2-STEP EMAIL OPT-IN LEAD GENERATION

The LeadPages funnel was so successful that we took its winning elements and created a smaller version of the page called a LeadBox. We put a new opt-in section on the eCommerce website that enticed people to download the bone broth recipe guide. We then ran the new opt-in area versus the original newsletter form opt-in, and the results were astounding. Not only did the new opt-in area triple e-mail collection results, but it also increased conversion rates by 14%. It was interesting to learn that visitors who were not interested in buying on the first visit were at least very interested in downloading the free recipe guide. This way we were at least getting the visitors onto the Wise Choice Market e-mail list.

TEST: ADD EMAIL OPT-IN BUTTONS TO LANDING PAGE

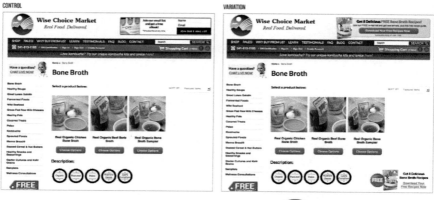

We then applied a similar LeadBox strategy to the mobile website because many e-commerce software companies now offer responsive websites. Responsive web design is an approach aimed at crafting sites that provide an optimal viewing experience—easy reading and navigation with minimal resizing, panning, and scrolling—across a wide range of devices from desktop computer monitors to mobile phones. It makes your website mobile friendly, but you need to customize the experience to generate leads and sales.

To do this for the WiseChoiceMarket website, we used a LeadBox for the homepage and all category pages, positioning it above the fold on all mobile devices. The problem with responsive design is that it compresses all of the information onto one page, resulting in the page being very long. This pushed the original footer email opt-in area out of the reach of the visitors. But by adding the "Download Free Recipes" LeadBox to their website, we increased their daily email collection on mobile devices from zero to seven emails per day, dramatically growing the email list which, in turn, worked to increase the mobile conversion rate.

TEST: MOBILE LEAD GENERATION

CONTROL   VARIATION

7x DAILY EMAIL OPT-IN FREQUENCY

Next we were able to move to the homepage, another area that had a huge amount of traffic but hadn't been optimized yet. We created a specific hypothesis for creating a new homepage. Now this homepage was a *big* change. It implemented new navigation elements and new homepage lead generation forms. There was lots of information going on there, so we wanted to figure out the best way to test it.

To do that, we broke the page up into different sections and started by testing it on the existing site. It took a lot of effort to make it work, but in the end, we saw a major increase in conversion rate and a major increase in average order value and overall customer satisfaction.

The next step for this client was to move what we'd learned on category, product pages, and the homepage into our paid advertising and lead generation. We were using different landing page software to figure out how to leverage existing wins and scale them to increase our bottom line. We were also using retargeting marketing campaigns with Facebook ads to send traffic to specific landing pages so we could segment our data and continue these steps to have even more impact.

This is just the beginning of the optimization process. In the long run, you'll eventually start to get diminishing returns, but in the short term, you're going to see big revenue increases and learn a lot about your customers. After six months, we determined that the conversion rates had increased more than 50%, and we had tripled their daily leads. In addition, sales were growing faster—and more steadily—than ever before.

We had reached a place where the site had been optimized to a point where we were ready to do a *full* redesign. Our next step was to create a new website taking into account everything we had learned. We planned to run the new site and old site parallel for a few months to test the conversion rates and get even more customer feedback.

In summary, by using the Marketing Optimization System, we were able to dramatically impact the bottom line results for WiseChoiceMarket.com. From June through August of 2014, they averaged 450 orders per month, and then in Jan of 2015 they had 1,384 sales. They also went from an average of 150 new customers per month in June through August to over 500 new customers per month in January. Plus, after implementing the new lead generation strategy, we helped increase their daily average of new e-mail opt-ins from three subscribers per day to an average of over fifty new e-mail opt-ins on a daily basis. Now all marketing campaigns can run more effectively using with the Marketing Optimization System.

To learn more about the results of this entire project, visit the website: SBBMO.com

TRIPLE YOUR SALES & LEADS

*"If you're not measuring,
you're not growing."*
~Alex Harris

Learn How You Can Triple Your Website Sales & Leads in Under Six Months

Adopting a well-planned marketing optimization system can help you *triple* your online sales in under six months.

The most opportunity is available if your websites have never been optimized before. This is where you can use website conversion secrets called Quick Wins. These are obvious changes that can have a huge impact based on your detailed research, which you will use to create a hypothesis for iterative experiments.

ITERATIVE EXPERIMENTS

QUALITATIVE

QUANTITATIVE

UVP & COPY

HYPOTHESIS

UX & M.A.P.

SCALE & GROW

The formula is a two-prong approach. First, stop buying additional website traffic and second, leverage your existing traffic to increase your conversion rates. Identify the top traffic landing pages on your website with revenue-generating opportunity. In the first month, you focus on finding all the quick wins for easy improvements. Then in months two through three, you will concentrate on all opportunities with high revenue potential. Month four is when you start focusing on quality traffic and lead generation. Reevaluate your paid traffic and remove non-converting paid ads. This will help to lower your CPA, cost per acquisition. As you test more and more, you should reach month five and be able to scale your wins to other marketing channels like social media and e-mail campaigns. Once you know what's working, you can increase your ppc budget and begin increasing lifetime value using e-mail marketing. After reading the case studies in this book, you will see how we first learned everything possible about the potential of the website and then validated using split testing.

TRIPLE YOUR SALES & LEADS IN UNDER 6 MONTHS

- ⊕ **TODAY:** Stop Buying Additional Traffic
- ⊕ **Month 1:** Convert Existing Traffic
- ⊕ **Month 2:** Highest Value (Revenue) Tests
- ⊕ **Month 3:** Highest Value (Revenue) Tests
- ⊕ **Month 4:** Lower CPA & Remove Bad Traffic
- ⊕ **Month 5:** Scale Wins to Lead Generation & Email
- ⊕ **Month 6:** Add Sales Team, PPC Budget & Affiliates

In month six, you should attain your local maximum. Local maximum is reached when you have realized the full conversion optimization potential of your existing websites. Once you reach this point, it may be a good time to redesign your website based on all of the research and learning you discovered during the Marketing Optimization Process.

To recap, the framework is comprised of three modules:

1. Customer Mindset
2. Gathering Intelligence
3. Marketing Optimization System

And the Marketing Optimization System is organized into three phases:

1. Strategic Evaluation
2. Five-Step Process
3. Bottom Line Growth Plan

To reiterate, the Marketing Optimization System is broken down into the following five steps, but we *always* start with a Strategic Evaluation and end with a Bottom Line Growth Plan.

1. Discovery
2. Hypothesis
3. Execution
4. Review
5. Scale

FINAL THOUGHTS

●●●●●●●●●●●●●●●●●●●

*Optimization is the art and science of
combining intuition with rigorous process
then testing to see what works.*

~Chris Goward, Founder of WiderFunnel and
Author of You Should Test That!

When you first started this book, you may have thought you knew everything about Internet marketing and running an online business. In this book, I'm giving you fresh ideas and encouraging you to think differently. Maybe this was your "Aha!" moment—maybe you now realize that your website could be making a whole lot more money than it has been. You see this often—it happens time and time again. Things are going so well for so long, and then you gear up for the holiday season but end up not having the results you expected. You had probably become complacent and took things for granted, thinking your conversion rates were going to remain steady, and you could just easily coast through your online success.

Maybe you have a pay-per-click (PPC) company managing your eCommerce or lead generation websites. They may have been a profitable marketing channel for you in the past, but advertising is now suddenly more expensive than ever, and in the end, when everything has been said and done, you might not be seeing the results you'd hoped for.

I understand how frustrating that can get. Which is exactly why *now* is the time to take your online marketing even more seriously. I'm here to help you take your business to the next level and show you how to make more money from your site.

The process I have outlined here may not work for you. I recommend evaluating your business and choosing a system that addresses your personal goals. Use it to create your own marketing optimization system. Whatever you do, have a system that works for you and continuously improve upon it. This will enable you to achieve more consistent results.

You can predict the future of your marketing and maximize your profit in a shorter period of time. You can predict the future of your marketing and get compound results.

I'd like to thank you for purchasing this book. There are thousands of books out there, but you took a chance and chose this one. As a special gift, be sure to grab your free workbook, videos and course at SBBMO.com

If you have any questions, please contact me by visiting my website AlexDesigns.com or by e-mailing me at alex@alexdesigns.com.

Your comments are very valuable because they will guide future editions of this book, and I'm always striving to improve.

And if you like what you've read, I need your help! Please take a minute to leave a quick review on Amazon.

Thanks so much!

REFERENCES

Eisenberg, Bryan. Eisenberg, Jeffrey. David, Lisa T. 2006. *Persuasive Online Copywriting.*

Eisenberg, Bryan. Quarto-vonTivadar, John. 2008. *Always Be Testing: The Complete Guide to Google Website Optimizer.*

Eisenberg, Bryan. 2011. BryanEisenberg.com, *The Conversion Trinity: The 3 Step Magic Formula to Increase Click Throughs & Conversions.* http://www.bryaneisenberg.com/the-conversion-trinity-the-3-step-magic-formula-to-increase-click-throughs-conversions/

Eisenberg, Bryan. 2012. BryanEisenberg.com, *Conversion Optimization 101: Ad Continuity/Scent.* http://www.bryaneisenberg.com/conversion-optimization-101-ad-continuityscent/

Eisenberg, Jeffrey. Eisenberg, Bryan. Garcia, Anthony. 2014. *Buyer Legends: The Executive Storyteller's Guide.*

Smith, Cooper. 2014. BusinessInsider.com, *Inside The Trillion-Dollar Battle to Recover ECommerce Sales Lost to Abandoned Shopping.* http://www.businessinsider.com/heres-how-retailers-can-reduce-shopping-cart-abandonment-and-recoup-billions-of-dollars-in-lost-sales-2014-9

Patel, Sujan. 2014. Forbes.com, *6 Predictions about the State of Digital Marketing in 2015.* http://www.forbes.com/sites/sujanpatel/2014/11/05/6-predictions-about-the-state-of-digital-marketing-in-2015/

Tommy Walker. 2014. *3 Frameworks to Help Prioritize & Conduct Your Conversion Testing.* http://conversionxl.com/3-frameworks-help-prioritize-conduct-conversion-testing/

Amanda Durepos. 2014. *How to Make Your Landing Page More Persuasive Using Buying Modalities.* http://unbounce.com/landing-pages/dissolving-friction-on-your-landing-page/

HOW TO REACH ALEX HARRIS

Hundreds of companies have used these methods to increase their online profits. Make this process work for *your* website, and grow your business faster. Now you can take advantage of this proven system to make more money. You will learn the tools that fit you and your site best. Make a dramatic impact on your bottom line by increasing your conversion rates for your existing website traffic.

You deserve it!

E-mail Alex at   :   alex@alexdesigns.com
Learn more at   :   AlexDesigns.com
Follow Alex on Twitter   :   twitter.com/alexdesigns
See photos on Instagram :   instagram.com/alexdesigns
Join Alex on Facebook   :   facebook.com/alexdesignsllc
Watch weekly videos   :   youtube.com/alexdesignsllc

Don't delay in contacting me. You deserve better results. I'm here to serve you, so feel free to ask any questions you want. It's my pleasure to help you rise to the next level in your business.

ABOUT THE AUTHOR

Alex graduated from Florida State University in 1998 and then worked as creative director at eDiets.com from 2000 to 2011. In 2004, he took what he learned and created AlexDesigns.com, an eCommerce consulting and web design company specializing in eCommerce, landing page design, conversion rate optimization, and marketing. As president, Alex's goal is to help clients get the best web design while helping them to increase online sales, generate more leads, and make more money.

Need a speaker for your seminar or conference? How about a group training workshop?

E-mail Alex at alex@alexdesigns.com

Learn more about Alex Harris. Visit AlexDesigns.com.

Made in the USA
Middletown, DE
16 January 2016